STO

SEP 6 '78

**ACPL ITEM
DISCARDED**

3 1833 04493 0953

 W9-DFT-483

the story of

DINOSAURS

A Guidebook for Young Scientists

by

Dr. Stanley B. Brown
School of Education
University of California,
Berkeley

Barbara M. Brown
Consultant,
Science Education

Reviewed for scientific accuracy by

Mary B. Patsuris *Department of Geology and Paleontology*

The American Museum of Natural History

designed and illustrated by

Don Bolognese

j560
B81s

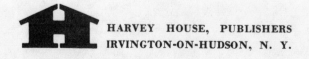
Harvey House, Publishers
Irvington-on-Hudson, N. Y.

© 1958 by
Z. E. HARVEY, INC.
Irvington-on-Hudson, N. Y.
All rights reserved, including
the right to reproduce this book
or portions thereof in any form.

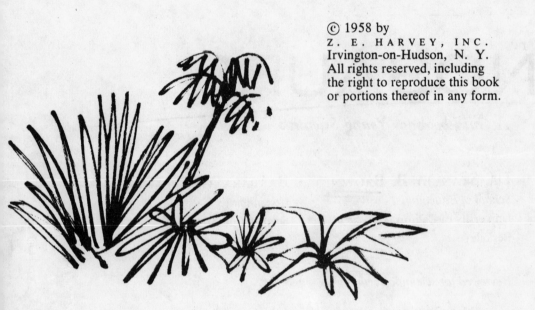

Library of Congress Catalog Card Number 58–13925

Manufactured in the U. S. A.

Contents

CO. SCHOOLS
C531087

1 *Introducing Dinosaurs*

Millions of years ago, in the Age of Reptiles, dinosaurs (DY-nuh-sawrs) were the ruling animals of the earth. Today man rules the earth. No man has ever seen a live dinosaur. All of these strange animals died millions of years before the first men lived.

The word dinosaur means "terrible lizard." This name was given to the first skeletons found over 100 years ago. At that time men knew very little about animals that no longer lived on the earth. As more fossil skeletons were found, these ancient animals had to be called something. The fossils looked like great, terrible lizards, and that is what they were named.

Some dinosaurs were the most fierce and terrible creatures you can imagine. The terrible dinosaurs were the flesh-eaters. Scientists call them carnivores (CAR-nih-vors). There were small ones no bigger than rabbits or chickens.

The biggest flesh-eater was **Tyrannosaurus rex** (tih-RAN-uh-SAWR-us rex) who lived near the end of the Age of Reptiles. He was more than forty-five-feet long and stood almost twenty feet tall—as high as a two-story house. His jaws were a yard in length

Biography

and filled with sharp dagger-like teeth. He moved about swiftly on powerful back legs, chasing other dinosaurs. When he caught one, the curved claws at the end of his tiny arms held the struggling animal while his great jaws tore out chunks of flesh almost as big as a man.

Many dinosaurs were harmless plant-eaters. Scientists call them herbivores (HERB-ih-vors). They were all sizes, too. One of the biggest plant-eaters was **Brontosaurus** (bront-uh-SAWR-us). **Brontosaurus** means "thunder lizard." Elephants are the biggest land-animals alive today. But **Brontosaurus** weighed more than ten elephants. He had a long tail, a long snake-like neck, and a very tiny head. Big plant-eaters like **Brontosaurus** spent most of their time in the water. They were harmless monsters. They moved quietly around in swamp waters feeding on tons of floating water plants every day. The water helped hold up their huge bodies and they came out on dry land only to bask in the warm sun or lay eggs. These plant-eaters walked on four legs.

Other big plant-eaters walked on two legs. These were the trachodonts (TRACK-uh-donnts) or duck-billed dinosaurs. They were huge but not quite so large as **Brontosaurus** or **Tyrannosaurus.** The trachodonts were about thirty feet long, and had broad, flat bills—just like ducks. They walked upright, balanced

by heavy tails. Trachodonts moved about more easily on land than their larger plant-eating cousins, but they liked the water, too. They were good swimmers. When hungry meat-eaters chased them, they probably swam fast for deep water where they could not be followed. These harmless plant-eaters had no other way to defend themselves.

There were other plant-eaters that stayed on dry land. But giant meat-eaters prowled through the jungles and the harmless dinosaurs had to develop ways to protect themselves. The plant-eating **Stegosaurus** (stegg-uh-SAWR-us) was one of the first of the armored dinosaurs. He was about twenty feet long. A double row of large flat plates grew on his back from his head to nearly the tip of his tail. Four long spikes at the end of his ten-foot tail were weapons of defense.

Brontosaurus

After the stegosaurs came more armored dinosaurs. Ankylo-saurs (ANG-kull-uh-SAWRS) looked something like walking army tanks. Their broad, flat bodies were covered with bony plates. Sometimes they had spikes sticking out at odd angles. Some of them looked like huge horned toads.

The last of the dinosaurs to come and go were the ceratopsians (serr-uh-TOPS-e-yunns) or horned dinosaurs. These reptiles were plant-eaters. They carried their armor on their heads. A wide bony frill or collar protected their necks. Long horns projected forward like spears attached to a warrior's shield. As long as they could keep such enemies as **Tyrannosaurus** in front of them, they probably lumbered quite safely through the jungles.

Large or small, fast or slow, two-legged or four-legged, meat-eating or plant-eating-dinosaurs were the most exciting animals

that ever lived on the earth. Dinosaurs were land animals even though some of them spent a great deal of time in or near the water.

The air and seas were filled with other reptiles almost as strange and terrible as the dinosaurs. Flying reptiles swooped through the air with twenty-foot wings. The seas and lakes swarmed with other reptiles. Some looked like fish. Others looked like long snakes strung through giant turtle bodies. And there were forty-foot sea lizards that thrashed the waters into white foam as they tried to snap off the three-foot heads of giant sea turtles.

The land, the sea, and the air were filled with frightening creatures in the Age of Reptiles.

Eras in Earth's History

CENOZOIC ERA

(SEE-nuh-ZO-ick)

Age of Mammals

MESOZOIC ERA

(MESS-uh-ZO-ick)

Age of Reptiles

PALEOZOIC ERA

(PAY-lee-uh-ZO-ick)

Age of Amphibians

Age of Fishes

**Age of Animals
without Backbones**

PROTEROZOIC ERA

(PROTT-wir-uh-ZO-ick)

Simple Forms of Life

ARCHEOZOIC ERA

(ARK-ee-uh-ZO-ick)

One-celled Forms of Life

1.1 The Age of Reptiles

Man has lived on the earth about one million years. That seems like a very long time. But it is a very short time when we think of the entire history of the earth.

Scientists believe the earth is at least two billion years old. All earth history is divided into eras. Each era has periods depending upon what happened on earth at a certain time. Scientists have given names to these eras and periods. You can think of them as parts of a book called the Earth's History. Each chapter is an era. Each section in a chapter is a period within that era.

We do not know how or when life began on the earth. For millions of years after the beginning of the earth there were no living things.

For millions of more years the first plants and animals had no hard parts that could be preserved in rock as fossils. This time is called the Proterozoic Era.

We do know that about 500 million years ago the first plants and animals lived that had hard parts which could be preserved as fossils. All life at that time was in the sea. The forms of life resembled crabs or sea shell animals. It was the Age of Invertebrates—animals without backbones.

Millions of years later backboned fishes lived in the seas— the Devonian Period, the Age of Fishes.

It took millions of more years before the first land animals developed from the fishes. Like the frogs, living today, these animals lived on land as well as in the water. Scientists called that period the Age of Amphibians (am-FIBB-ih-yunns).

Over millions of more years, the first reptiles evolved from the amphibians. And so we come to the time in Earth History when the dinosaurs lived—the Age of Reptiles.

In our short story of Earth History we have traveled quickly through the following eras:

Some 1500 million years including the Archeozoic (ARK-ee-uh-ZO-ick) and the Proterozoic (PROTT-urr-uh-ZO-ick) Eras.

Some 350 million years of the Paleozoic (PAY-lee-uh-ZO-ick) Era that includes the periods called:

Cambrian (KAMM-brih-yunn)

Ordovician (or-doe-VISH-yunn)

Silurian (sih-LURE-ih-yunn)

Devonian (deh-VOH-nih-yunn)

Mississippian

Pennsylvanian

Permian (PURR-mih-yunn)

It has taken us only a few minutes to skip over about eighteen-hundred million years of Earth History. Now we have reached the Mesozoic (mess-uh-ZO-ick) Era, the Age of Reptiles and the days of dinosaurs.

The Age of Reptiles began some 200 million years ago and ended about 60 million years ago. Dinosaurs were everyday animals, like man today, for some 140 million years. The last dinosaur disappeared about 59 million years before the first man appeared on earth.

During the last part of the Age of Reptiles, small furry mammals began to scurry through the forests. Mammals became the rulers of the earth after the death of all the dinosaurs.

Cycads

All of this happened very slowly. It is not easy to think of millions of years. The first ape-like human beings began to live more than one million years ago. The written history of man goes back a short 7000 years. But the time back to dinosaurs is very, very long indeed.

1.2 What the Earth was Like

The earth was much different during the Age of Reptiles from what it is now. Today we have areas on the earth that are warm all year round. Other places are cold all year around. But during the Age of Reptiles the climate was the same almost everywhere. The year-round warm, moist climate made it possible for cold-blooded reptiles to wander over the earth to areas where they could not live today. Because the climate over most of the earth was ideal for reptiles, they lived and flourished.

It was so warm during the Age of Reptiles that forests of fig trees, cinnamon trees and tree ferns grew almost as far north as the North Pole. Swamps and lowlands were filled with soft, juicy plants. Thick jungles of palm-like trees and cycads (SY-kads) covered the drier lands. Cycads are stubby trees somewhat like palms and ferns. Toward the end of the Mesozoic era familiar trees like walnuts, magnolias, sycamores, and sequoias appeared.

13

Seas were spread over many areas that are now dry land. The state of Kansas was under water. At times, Wyoming, Montana, and Colorado were also covered with seas. The land changed often during 140 million years. It lifted in places and the seas flowed away. The land dried and then these places would sink and the waters would flow over them again.

Some of the great mountain ranges that we know today were not yet born during the Age of Reptiles. There were no Himalayas or Rocky Mountains. An inland sea covered the area where the Rocky Mountains are now.

Scientists believe that land bridges connected the continents. The dinosaurs could roam across land from what is now Asia to North America. North and South America were probably con-

NORTH AMERICA   TRIASSIC PERIOD

14

nected by more land than they are today. Europe and Africa met across the Mediterranean Sea. What is now the East Indies was a land bridge from Australia to Asia. Perhaps even North America and Europe were connected across Iceland and Greenland. You can see why dinosaurs roamed freely. The oceans, mountains and cold climates of today did not exist then to prevent the reptiles from moving about.

Dinosaur bones are found on every continent. The story of dinosaurs has been pieced together from bones, teeth and other fossils dug out of rocks that have been exposed. Scientists have found the remains of many different kinds. Perhaps a great many more kinds of dinosaurs are still hidden deep in the rock layers beneath the surface of the earth.

NORTH AMERICA — CRETACEOUS PERIOD

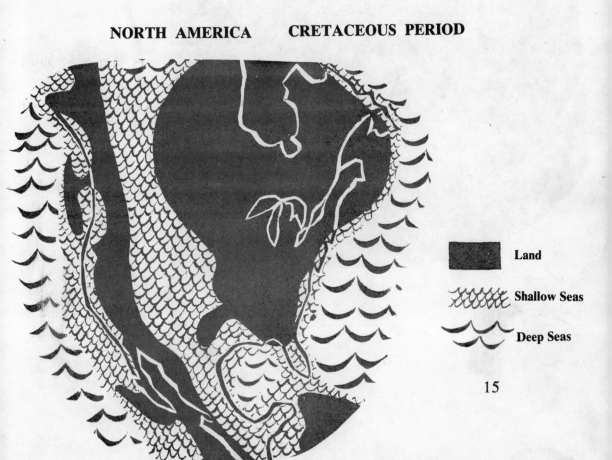

Land

Shallow Seas

Deep Seas

15

2   The Story Told By Rocks

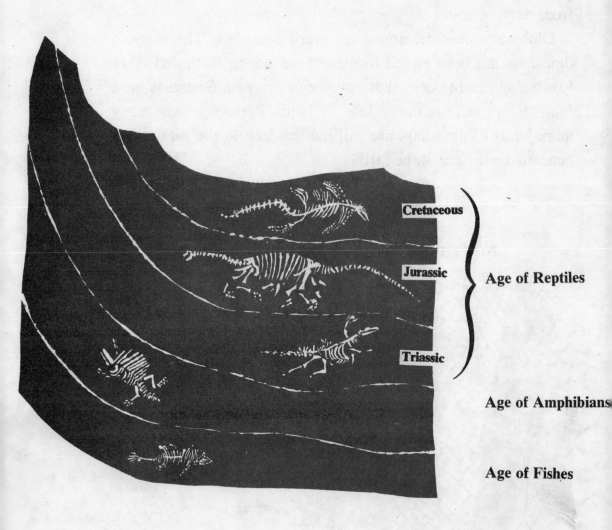

Cretaceous

Jurassic — Age of Reptiles

Triassic

Age of Amphibians

Age of Fishes

The story of the dinosaurs took place millions of years before any people lived on the earth. Their story has been pieced together in the same way a detective solves a mystery. Scientists look for clues in rocks to solve the mystery of past life on the earth.

No matter where you dig on the earth, if you dig far enough you will come to solid rock. Sometimes the rock is covered with water, sometimes with soil. Other times you do not have to dig at all because the solid rock comes right to the surface.

In places like Grand Canyon or along roads in the mountains you can see layers of different kinds of rocks. There are hundreds of different kinds of rocks making up the earth's crust. Some rocks were formed in one way, others in another. Scientists have studied how rocks are made. They can tell what was happening on earth when the different layers of rock were formed.

Some rock layers tell about the oceans of long ago. Some tell about volcanic lava flows of ancient times. Some tell of changes in the climate, and others tell how mountains were made.

Fossils are found in some rock layers. Fossils tell about plants and animals that lived long ago. So, some layers of rock tell several stories at one time. They tell where the dry land and oceans were, what kinds of plants and animals lived then, and what changes were taking place.

This is not so simple as it sounds. Scientists all over the world have to work together to piece all the clues into a complete story of the earth.

Some times the earth pushed upward in places, and rock layers were worn away by wind, rain, and rivers. Where the earth again sank new layers covered the worn away rocks. So scientists sometimes find that parts of the earth's history have been worn away.

In other places the earth's crust was folded over. Sometimes the older layers of rock may be folded on top of the newer ones.

At the end of the Age of Reptiles there were volcanic eruptions in the western part of our country and the Rocky Mountains began to push up. If you visit Boulder, Colorado on the eastern side of the Rocky Mountains you can see the Flatirons. They are layers of rock sticking almost straight up in the air. This Rocky Mountain area was once flat and the home of dinosaurs. Fossils found in the rocks there prove it.

2.1 How Fossils Are Formed

Fossils are the remains of plants or animals of long ago that were buried under mud or sand. If conditions were just right and the remains were preserved, a fossil formed. There are many kinds of fossils, just as there are many kinds of rocks.

Plant Fossils

One kind of fossil is a petrified (stony) bone, tooth, or shell. Often when an animal dies, its body is destroyed by other animals. But sometimes the body will be quickly covered by the mud of a shallow river, the ooze at the bottom of the ocean, or by shifting desert sands. Water containing minerals seeps through the mud or sand where the animal is buried. Slowly, the pores and spaces in the bone are completely filled in by various minerals. It is petrified. Most of the dinosaur skeletons we see in museums are this kind of fossil. A bone can be petrified in a few hundred years if conditions are right and the water is heavy with minerals. Or it may take thousands of years to petrify.

The same thing can happen to plants. The Petrified Forest in Arizona is a place where hundreds of stone trees lie on the ground.

18

The vegetable matter in these trees was completely replaced by minerals. You can see the forms of wood cells with a microscope.

Sometimes a fossil may be the hard part of an animal that has not been completely changed to stone. These are called "sub-fossils." Either these fossils are not too old, or conditions for turning to stone were such that they were never entirely mineralized.

Some fossils may be found as molds. Many fine impressions of plants and insects have been found in "paper-shales." This kind of rock was made from very fine bits of matter desposited in flat layers. The layers separate into sheets as thin as paper. Insects or leaves fell upon the surface of quiet water and sank to the bottom of the pool. They were gently covered with very fine mud. As the mud dried and the animal or plant matter decayed, an exact mold was left. Often molds of plants or animals can be found between the thin sheets of sandstone or shale.

If the mold is filled with mud or sand which has turned to stone, we call it a cast. A cast shows us the outer shape of the ancient plant or animal. It tells us nothing about the inside structure. Many sea shell animals, birds' eggs, or nuts are preserved this way.

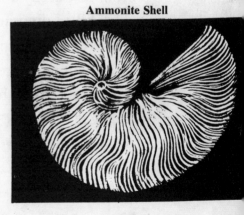

Ammonite Shell

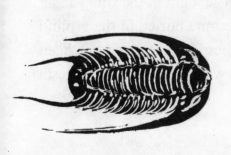

Trilobite

Brachiopod

Another kind of fossil is a track, a footprint, or even the marks left by a leaf brushing across mud. Perhaps a dinosaur walked across a muddy area and left his heavy tracks. As time went by, sand or more mud washed into these depressions and did not change their shape. Slowly the sediments turned into stone and the footprints were preserved.

Prints of this kind have been found in Texas, Montana, and Connecticut. Areas like these may have been river beds or shallow arms of the sea. They would be covered with water for a while, and then baked dry in the hot sun for days or weeks. Later, the muddy water would wash over them again.

Dinosaur tracks of this kind are important. They show how the dinosaurs walked. Some tracks show that certain dinosaurs "sat" on their thick tails to rest or balance themselves. Others, found in Texas, show the trails of many dinosaurs crossing sandbars. The marks of what might be baby dinosaurs can be seen following along with the big ones. There are foot-prints of flesh-eating dinosaurs stalking the herds of plant-eaters. We learn many things about the world of long ago from dinosaur tracks.

Fossils of whole animals or insects have been found in which even the soft parts are fossilized. The soft parts were protected from fast decay and minerals quickly seeped in. The imprint of a duck-billed dinosaur's skin has been found this way.

Fossils have also been found of insects caught in the sticky resin of ancient pine trees. Later the resin became buried in the ground and turned to amber. The bodies of these insects have not been changed and look exactly as they did when trapped in the resin some 25 million years ago.

Some fossils were filled with such unusual minerals as opal. In the Gobi Desert, the skeleton of a dinosaur was found in which the pores and spaces in the bones had been completely filled with iron.

There are other kinds of fossils, too. The La Brea Tar Pits in southern California trapped many kinds of animals as they stumbled into this soft area and were not able to get out. Other fossils have been found frozen in ice near the North Pole.

Fossil skeletons tell how the animals looked. Footprints tell something about their habits. Impressions of wood, leaves, and seeds tell what those plants looked like. Plant fossils even tell a story of the climate. Palm tree and cycad fossils tell that the climate was warm and with much rain. If trees and plants were of a desert type, the climate was dry. Fossils are like written words in the rock-layer pages of earth's history.

2.2 Finding Fossils

The first thing a dinosaur hunter must know is where to begin looking for fossils. Only in sedimentary rocks like limestone, sandstone, shale or slate will you find fossils. These rocks are formed by fine mud or sand pressed together. Fossils cannot be found in granite or volcanic rocks.

Dinosaurs lived during the Mesozoic era. So their remains will be found in sedimentary rocks of the Mesozoic era, and nowhere else.

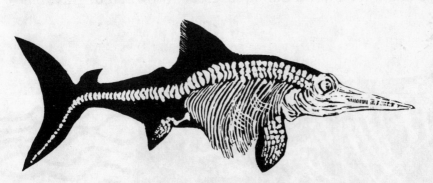

Ichthyosaur

21

In the early days, fossil hunting was a hit and miss affair. Rock layers were not well known nor well mapped. Now most areas in the world have been studied. Rocks have been mapped in such a way that scientists know where to look for the fossils they want.

The best place to hunt fossils is where rivers have cut the land into valleys with steep sides. This exposes the edges of the rock layers and gives a cross-sectional picture of the land. It would be foolish for a fossil hunter to start digging in the middle of a flat field and hope to find fossils in the rocks below.

Dinosaur bones are often found in ancient swamp areas or in mud flats where ancient rivers met the seas. Scientists say that thousands of wonderful fossils may be hidden beneath the surface of the earth. But fossil hunters have to let nature do some of the digging for them. Usually these nature-dug areas are in desert or dry country. In such places there are few trees, grass, or other plants to protect the soil from erosion by rain or wind. Flash floods that cut deep gullies into the earth sometimes expose bones buried in the rock layers.

After the dinosaur hunter picks out an area where the rocks are right for finding dinosaur bones, he follows a step-by-step plan.

First he looks for the rock layers which should have the fossils he wants. Then he "walks out" this layer looking for bits of bone. He learns to see fossils that we would probably miss. A tiny piece of bone might look like a dull blue, green, brown, red, gray, black

or gleaming white stone to us. But the scientist can sometimes sit at quite a distance and, with a pair of binoculars, spot a dinosaur bone by its shape or color sticking out of rock. Such a method is for experts, only.

This is just the beginning of the work. Getting the bones out of the rock is a long and hard task. Sometimes tons of heavy rock above the fossil must be taken away. Fossil hunters use picks, shovels, and hammers. Once in a while dynamite may be needed to loosen the fossils from their rock beds. Carefully the fossil hunter chips the rock away to see how big the fossil is. He takes photographs to show just how the bones were found.

After the top rock is chipped and whisked away, each piece of the skeleton is painted with shellac and covered with tissue paper so it will not crumble to powder.

If the bones are easy to get out of the rock, they are taken out one by one. If many bones are jumbled together, the whole block of rock may be chipped out. The block is covered with the shellac and paper.

To protect each piece further, the bone or block of rock is covered with strips of burlap dipped in a flour paste or liquid plaster. The burlap and paste covering hardens and forms a strong cast over the bones. The fossil can then be moved without breaking. It is like a cast the doctor puts on a broken arm or leg.

When the fossil gets to the museum, workers carefully take off the burlap and plaster cast. Then the fossil is cleaned. Very carefully the remaining rock is chipped away from the bone.

After this work is done, the scientist examines the fossil, compares it with other fossils, and tries to identify it. If it is a new kind of fossil, he writes about it in a scientific magazine so that students and scientists all over the world can read about it.

Only clearly identified fossils are placed in museums where we can see them. The rest are kept stored in back rooms of the museum for further study.

Large skeletons need a great deal more work to make them ready for museum showing. Iron rods are bent to support the bones and the skeleton is hung on iron frames. Several people may work together on this task so that the pose is true to life and

Diplodocus

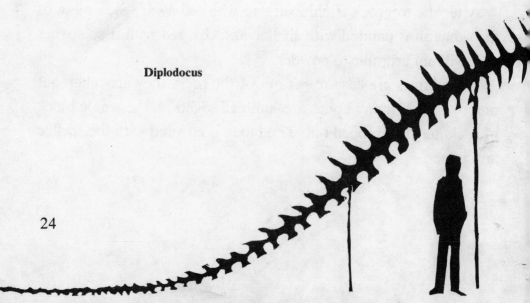

interesting for us to see. It is so skillfully done that sometimes we have to look hard to see how a big skeleton of a **Diplodocus** is held together. Sometimes models are made to show us how the dinosaur looked when it was alive.

Signs must be made to tell us about the dinosaurs. Also a picture is painted to show how the dinosaur looked in real life. The artist and scientist work together to give as true a picture as possible of an animal that no one has seen. Fossils of plants or other animals that lived at the same time as the dinosaur are painted to tell us how the earth looked at that time. Now the picture is ready for us to see.

This is the story of the fossil, from finding it in its rock bed to its place in the museum where we see it.

All we know about dinosaurs we have learned from fossils. Their bones tell us about their size, how they looked and some things they did. Fossil bones also tell us how the different dinosaurs were related to one another. Fossils in older rocks tell us about dinosaurs' ancestors and how the different kinds developed over the years.

3   Early Dinosaur Hunters

About a hundred years ago, the science of paleontology (PAY-lee-yonn-TAHL-uh-jee), the study of past life on our earth, was just beginning. At that time, scientists knew very little about digging out, preserving, and identifying fossils. Workmen sometimes came across strange fossils in rock quarries where they were cutting roof slates or building blocks. These fossils would be roughly chipped out and passed on to professors to study and to try to identify.

Because no one knew too much about fossils, the bits of bones would often end up in storerooms. People thought the bones belonged to some unknown animals. But more and more fossils were found and men became more and more interested in them.

Some men began to think that we could learn a great deal about the past life on earth from the bones found in rocks. But they felt that bits of bones or teeth found here or there did not tell the whole story. They needed more fossils in order to get a better picture of ancient life. And so these men started to search in earnest.

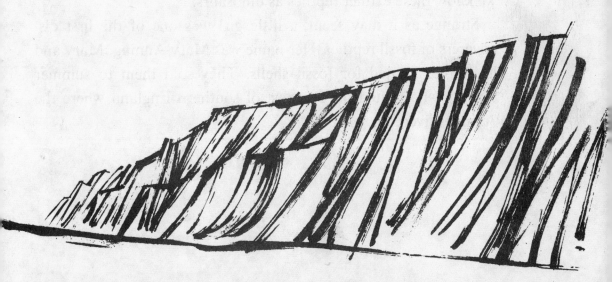

Now some sort of system had to be worked out for naming and studying fossils. One of the first men to do this was a Frenchman named, Baron Georges Cuvier (1769-1832). This great man may be called the founder of the science of Vertebrate Paleontology, the study of animals that had backbones and lived in the distant past. Cuvier was the first person to show how backboned animals were related. He gave future scientists a system for studying this kind of animal.

While Cuvier was working in France, Dr. Gideon Mantell in England was also looking for fossil remains in rocks. In 1822, his wife found some strange-looking teeth in rocks near Sussex, England. Several professors believed that these might be the teeth of a rhinoceros.

This explanation did not satisfy Dr. Mantell. He returned to the place where the teeth had been found. There he discovered several bones which looked like those of a large reptile. He named the animal **Iguanodon** (ih-GWANN-uh-dunn) because the teeth resembled those of the Iguana lizard that lives on the Galapagos Islands.

Up to this time, the fossil remains of these ancient reptiles had no general name. Then Sir Richard Owen made up the name Dinosauria, which as you know means "terrible lizards." Today we know these extinct reptiles as dinosaurs.

Strange as it may seem, a little girl was one of the first discoverers of fossil reptiles. Her name was Mary Anning. Mary and her father hunted for fossil shells. They sold them to summer tourists who visited the seacoast of southern England where the Annings lived.

28

Mary made a great discovery when she was twelve years old. In 1811, while looking for shells, she discovered the first fossil skeleton of an ancient sea reptile. This animal lived in the sea when the terrible lizards roamed the earth. The animal was named **Ichthyosaurus** (ICKTH-ee-uh-SAWR-us) which means fish-lizard.

Mary's discovery was great news to scientists. From that time on she searched for more skeletons. She continued to look for fossil shells, too, for the tourist trade, but she was more interested in the large skeletons.

In 1821, Mary found the first skeleton of a **Plesiosaurus** (PLEE-see-uh-SAWR-us), another sea reptile. And in 1828, she discovered the first flying reptile skeleton ever to be found in England, a pterosaur (TERR-uh-sawr). Pterosaur means wing-lizard. Mary Anning became famous in science for the many discoveries she made. She sold fossil skeletons to museums all over the world.

Fossil hunters found not only dinosaur bones and teeth but something else, too. At about the same time Cuvier and Mantell were working in Europe, dinosaur footprints were discovered in the Connecticut Valley.

As early as 1802 a farmer named Pliny Moody had noticed small bird-like imprints on a block of stone. These imprints were soon called the tracks of Noah's Raven. They were curious markings, but nobody got excited about them. In 1835 Professor Edward Hitchcock of Amherst College began to collect and study these tracks. He thought they had been made by some extinct bird. But he was wrong. They were dinosaur tracks.

Professor Hitchcock was one of the first collectors of dinosaur remains in our country, even though he did not know exactly what he had found. We understand his mistake because at that time no one knew much about dinosaurs. These three-toed marks did look like bird tracks.

The first dinosaur skeleton discovered in the United States came from the little town of Haddonfield, New Jersey, near Philadelphia. Workmen found the fossil remains while digging in the crumbling clay and shell deposits called a marl bed. The strange bones were carted off to various homes as souvenirs and used for doorstops or mantel decorations.

In 1858, some years later, Mr. W. Parker Foulke heard of this amazing discovery. He reopened the spot where the first bones

were found and dug out a great deal more of the skeleton. These fossil remains were placed in the Philadelphia Academy of Natural Sciences. There Dr. Joseph Leidy (1891-1923), who was the founder of the science of Paleontology in North America, studied the bones. He tracked down many of the souvenirs being used as door stops and decorations and put together the first skeleton of a duck-billed dinosaur, **Hadrosaurus** (had-ruh-SAWR-us). **Hadrosaurus** means "heavy lizard."

Not much was done in our country in the way of collecting and studying fossils until after the Civil War. Then the great territory of the West was opened. The United States Government started a series of "Territorial Surveys" of the West. Exploring parties needed geologists, the earth scientists. They could study this "new" land. And the geologists discovered many places rich in fossils.

Two American professors, Cope of Philadelphia and Marsh of Yale, became very much interested in the exciting new areas. At that time, from 1870 to 1895, the west was still wild. These two paleontologists sent out groups to the Great Plains and the Rocky Mountain basins to collect fossils.

Cope and Marsh started to compete with each other to see who could bring back the most specimens. Soon they were bitter enemies. Both men worked very hard. Two great collections were built up and dinosaurs formed a great part of them. These men found new ways of collecting, preparing, and studying fossils. They also interested the scientists and the museums throughout the world and expeditions started to go out and search for fossils. Today, there are museums all over the world that have fine collections of dinosaurs and other fossils.

Collecting parties roamed over the vast lands of Wyoming, Colorado, Kansas, Montana, Arizona, Texas and Alberta, Canada. A skeleton of the great **Brontosaurus** was discovered in a place called Bone Cabin Quarry in Wyoming.

Collections were also made in Asia, the Gobi Desert of Mongolia, and in the Karroo desert in South Africa. The American Museum of Natural History in New York now has a collection of dinosaurs and other fossil reptiles that is the best in the world.

Early in the 20th Century, the Andrew Carnegie Museum in Pittsburgh uncovered a large deposit of dinosaurs near Vernal, Utah. This place is now called the Dinosaur National Monument. It has a fine display of dinosaur remains. One wall of the canyon is part of the museum. You can lean over the guard rail in the

museum and watch the men at work. There you will see exactly
what the fossil bones look like in the rock when the scientists first
find them.

In the early time of fossil hunting, people were afraid that some-
day there would be no more fossils to find. But now it seems that
the supply is endless. New fields of fossils are always being found.

Great areas of rock still lie hidden below the surface of the
earth. They have not been worn away by streams nor dug into by
industrial workers. These areas may hold the remains of strange
dinosaurs that we know nothing about today. The hunt for dinosaurs and other fossils will go on where the great finds have already
been made. And the hunt is spreading to all parts of the earth,
wherever men think they can discover something new.

Early Lobe-finned Fish

4   Ancestors of Dinosaurs

As we go along, you will see how dinosaurs developed over the 140 million years of the Age of Reptiles—from the earliest to the last forms that lived. But first let's find out what the ancestors of dinosaurs were like.

4.1 Amphibians

About 500 million years ago plants and animals first developed hard body parts that could turn into fossils. All life was in the sea. No backboned animals lived. Most of the animals had shells or were crab-like forms.

The first backboned animals were fishes. There were many of them in the waters by the middle of the Paleozoic Era which was millions of years before the Age of Reptiles.

There were many kinds of fish. Some were large and some small. Some were fast, streamlined hunters and others were flattened grovelers and burrowers in the mud at the bottom of shallow seas.

34

A group of lobe-finned fishes called crossopterygians (cross-opp-tuh-RIDJ-e-yunns) were the direct ancestors of the first land-living back-boned animals. They were medium-sized animals, with bones in their fins. These bones were arranged like the limbs of their descendants, the first land-living vertebrates.

Of special interest to paleontologists was the recent discovery of a strange water animal. Scientists identified it as a living lobe-finned fish, name **coelacanth** (SEE-luh-kanth). It was caught off the coast of Africa. Lobe-finned fish lived during the Devonian period, the Age of Fishes. They seemed to have disappeared in the late Cretaceous period. Paleontologists thought the coelacanths had been extinct for about 60 million years along with the dinosaurs. A living coelacanth is a very important discovery.

CO. SCHOOLS
C531087

Coelacanth

One of the greatest events in the earth's history, came about when vertebrates, or backboned animals, started to leave the water to live on land. Some crossopterygian fishes struggled onto land and became the first amphibians. Amphibian (amm-FIBB-ih-yunn) means "two ways of life." They spent part of their lives in water and part on land.

35

But certain things had to change.

Water helps hold up a fish's body. A land animal must have a body that can support itself against the downward pull of gravity.

A fish breathes by gills and takes oxygen from the water. A land animal must breathe air through lungs.

The tail of a fish helps it swim, and the fins balance the body. In a land animal the fins become four legs, which must move the animal along, and the tail balances the body.

Fish live and hatch their eggs in water. But the new amphibians had not changed enough to lay their eggs on dry land. They had to return to the water.

Amphibians are cold-blooded land animals. Like fishes, they lay tiny jelly-like eggs. Each egg stores only a little food. It would soon dry up out of water because it has no shell to protect it. The young hatch in water and breathe with gills. As the young grow they develop lungs and can live on land.

Most of us have watched tadpoles grow into frogs or toads. Frogs, salamanders, and toads are amphibians. They can be traced back nearly to the beginning of the Age of Reptiles, and they look much the same now as they did then.

Diplocaulus

Amphibians today live harmlessly and quietly along streams or ponds. But when they first appeared they were kings of the land.

Labyrinthodonts (labb-uh-RINN-thoh-donnts) were large amphibians. The first ones looked like fish with short legs. They lived mostly in the water.

Later labyrinthodonts spent more time on land and grew into huge forms, like **Eryops** (ERR-ee-ops), with very strong legs.

For some reason, still later labyrinthodonts returned to water living. The earliest reptiles lived along with the amphibian labyrinthodonts. There was probably much elbowing around because these animals had to live close to the water and had to fight for space along the edges of swamps. Perhaps the new reptiles were better fitted for land living, and the labyrinthodonts had to retreat into the water.

The last forms of labyrinthodonts developed flattened bodies and heads. Their legs became weaker because they went back to a life in the water. The labyrinthodonts became extinct at the end of the first part of the Age of Reptiles.

Diplocaulus (dip-luh-KAWL-us) was one of the most interesting-looking amphibians. His body was flat and wide and his head was arrow-shaped.

Eryops

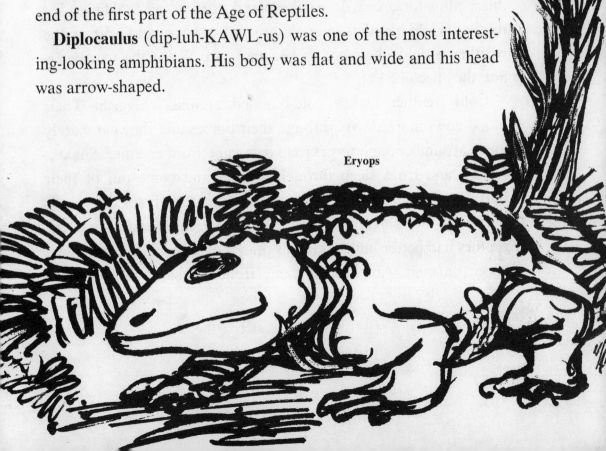

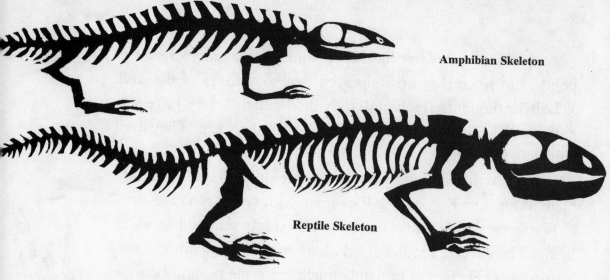

Amphibian Skeleton

Reptile Skeleton

4.2 Early Reptiles

The labyrinthodonts did become extinct. Yet a certain kind of labyrinthodont turned into the first of the reptiles.

The word reptile means "creeping animal." The first reptiles had a good deal in common with amphibians. But reptiles also had some differences that made them more successful as land animals.

Like fish and amphibians, the reptiles were cold-blooded. Crocodiles, alligators, lizards, snakes, and turtles are cold-blooded reptiles. Cold-blooded animals are not always cold. When the weather is cold, their bodies become cold. When the weather is hot, they become hot.

Cold weather makes cold-blooded animals sluggish. Their blood flows more slowly through their bodies and they can barely move around enough to get food or escape from enemies. Snakes, turtles, and frogs sleep through winters and come out of their burrows when the spring sun begins to warm their bodies.

Reptiles are different from amphibians in three ways. First, the reptiles had better-built skeletons than the amphibians for moving about on land. Amphibians came from fishes. Their short legs stuck out from the sides of their bodies and they crawled around slowly on their bellies. They looked like fish with legs. Early reptiles were something like this, too. But from these first reptiles, which still looked like amphibians, a new kind of reptile developed. This new reptile could lift its body and run on its hind legs. The legs grew from under the body instead of sticking out from the sides.

The second difference between reptiles and amphibians was in the skin. Amphibians often have a thin, smooth, and moist skin that dries in the air and sun. That's why amphibians must live near water. Reptiles developed a thicker skin, sometimes with scales, plates, and bony armor. It allowed the reptile to live comfortably on dry land. The thick, tough skin helped protect the animal against dryness, sun, and from enemies.

The third difference was the most important. It was the kind of egg the reptile laid. The tiny amphibian eggs do not have hard shells. The eggs must be laid and hatched in the water, too, because the young do not have lungs.

A reptile egg has a large yolk to feed the young before it hatches. It also has a membrane to protect the young reptile. The egg has a hard covering and can be laid on dry land. Air gets in through tiny holes, called pores, in the shell. A breathing organ carries the air to the young and lungs develop. When the baby hatches, it is ready to breathe on land. All reptiles breathe through lungs.

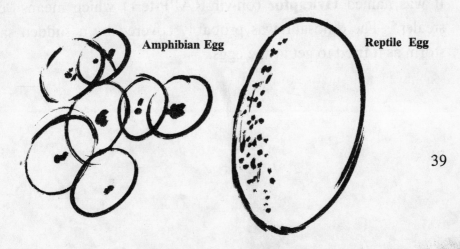

Amphibian Egg   **Reptile Egg**

39

This better development of the egg made reptiles the most important animals on earth for about 140 million years. Since the eggs could be laid on land, the reptiles were free to wander where they wished. They did not have to return to water to lay eggs. The young grew strong on the food stored in the yolk of the eggs before they hatched. That's why the young of most reptiles are not so helpless as most baby amphibians.

It took scientists a long time to prove that dinosaurs laid eggs. For a long time they did not know. Nobody had ever seen a dinosaur egg. Some people thought dinosaurs laid eggs as reptiles do today, but there was no proof.

In 1921, the American Museum of Natural History in New York City sent an expedition to collect fossils in the Gobi Desert in Mongolia. There, scientists found the first dinosaur fossil eggs. They found whole nests of eggs just as the female dinosaurs had laid them in circles millions of years ago.

The first dinosaur eggs found were about eight inches long and bluntly pointed at both ends. Most reptile eggs are shaped this way because they are laid in holes scooped in sand. It is said that bird's eggs are round at one end and pointed at the other so they will not roll out of nests.

The scientists found dinosaur bones near the eggs. A skeleton of a three-foot long dinosaur with no teeth was found close to the nest. It probably lived by sucking the eggs of other dinosaurs. It was named **Oviraptor** (oh-vih-RAPP-terr) which means "egg stealer." The dinosaur was probably covered by a sudden sand storm as it tried to get at the eggs.

40

Several years later the same scientists went back to the Gobi Desert and found more eggs of different kinds of dinosaurs. Some eggs were small, some bigger, and some had pebbled shells. Inside several of the fossil eggs they found the unhatched skeletons of baby dinosaurs. Here was the proof that dinosaurs laid eggs.

The Gobi Desert is the only place where dinosaur eggs have been found. It was probably dry, sandy, and warm millions of years ago—just right for dinosaur nests.

Dinosaurs did not "sit" on eggs like chickens. The mother dinosaur scooped out a shallow hole and laid her eggs. She then put a thin layer of sand over them. The sun warmed them. Probably the fossil eggs in the Gobi Desert were covered by a sudden sandstorm. The sand heaped over the nests and cut out the air and warmth for the babies inside the shell.

As the sand got heavier the eggs cracked and the liquid ran out. Sand sifted into the shell, helping the shell and the baby skeletons to keep their shapes. After thousands of years the sand was pressed into rock. After millions of years the rock was worn away and the scientists found the fossil eggs.

To get back to the early reptiles. The most common of the early reptiles were the cotylosaurs (KOTT-ih-luh-SAWRS). Cotylosaur means "cup-lizard." Many kinds developed. Most of them were small, or medium-sized, crawling, four-legged reptiles that looked like big lizards.

Cotylosaur

From the cotylosaurs, with amphibian-like skulls, all other groups of reptiles developed—the flying reptiles, sea reptiles and the dinosaurs. Today's snakes, turtles, lizards, and crocodiles have come from cotylosaurs. Scientists have also traced mammals and birds back through generations of ancestors to these same reptiles—the cotylosaurs.

4.3 Mammal-like Reptiles

The cotylosaurs did not have the world all to themselves. All through the story of life on the earth—the old, the in-between, and the new forms of animals overlapped. If you think of it in terms of a family, there would be grandfathers and grandchildren living side by side.

A fierce struggle took place on land between the labyrinthodonts, the cotylosaurs, and the newer reptiles. The labyrinthodonts were already disappearing. The cotylosaurs were competing with the many new kinds of reptiles and they, too, were doomed to die out. The same thing happened with the great dinosaurs millions of years later—they gave way to the mammals.

Some of the new reptiles were the ancestors of the warm-blooded, furry mammals. Cotylosaur became extinct, yet a branch of its family went on to become rulers of the earth.

Cynognathus (sih-NOGG-nuh-thuss) was an odd-looking creature, and a mammal-like reptile. **Cynognathus** means "dog jaw." He was a flesh-eater. But more important, he was one of a group of animals that spanned the bridge between the cold-blooded reptiles and the warm-blooded mammals.

42

Cynognathus

4.4 Thecodonts

At the beginning of the Age of Reptiles many changes were taking place in the different animals. The last of the labyrinthodont amphibians were moving back into ponds and streams. The mammal-like reptiles were roaming over the land looking for food.

About 25 million years had passed since the first cotylosaur came into being. These reptiles had branched out into several different kinds. One branch became the thecodonts (THEEK-uh-donnts). Thecodont means "socketed tooth." The thecodonts were the direct ancestors of the dinosaurs. They were also the ancestors of crocodiles and the flying reptiles.

The thecodonts were different from earlier reptiles in several ways. Their skulls were not so heavy. They had teeth along the edges of their jaws as we do. Most of the reptiles before them also had teeth covering the inside top of their mouths.

The thecodonts were different in still another way. They walked on two legs instead of four. They could run very fast. The two front legs grew shorter and turned into "hands" with sharp claws for grasping things. A long tail helped to balance the body and the head was lifted high in the air. They were meat-eaters and swift hunters.

These were the ancestors of the dinosaurs. The changing from one type of animal into another took millions of years. Now we come to the true dinosaurs.

Thecodont

Bird-like Hipped Dinosaurs

Trachodon

Triceratops

Styracosaurus

Corythosaurus

Monoclonius

Iguanodon

Ankylosaurus

Protoceratops

Camptosau

Stegosaurus

44

Thecodont

Tyrannosaurus rex

Struthiomimus

Allosaurus

Brontosaurus

Ornitholestes

Plateosaurus

5   *Kinds of Dinosaurs*

All of the dinosaurs descended from certain thecodont reptiles. When the name dinosaur was given to these ancient reptiles a hundred years ago, little was known about them. After scientists found and studied more fossils, they discovered that the dinosaurs were two groups of reptiles instead of just one.

They found that way back in Triassic (try-ASS-ick) days, some 200 million years ago when the Age of Reptiles was just beginning, the thecodonts split into two different groups.

We still call both groups dinosaurs. Some people like to divide dinosaurs into two groups—plant-eaters and meat-eaters. Some people divide them into two-legged and four-legged dinosaurs. Other people separate them into such groups as armored, horned, flying, and marine dinosaurs.

But the only right way to separate the dinosaurs is into the two groups scientists use. They separate them by the differences in their skeletons—especially in the hip bones. Scientists call one group of dinosaurs saurischians (sawr-ISS-kee-yunns) because they have lizard-like hip bones. The other group is called ornithischians (or-nih-THISK-e-yunns) because they have bird-like hip bones.

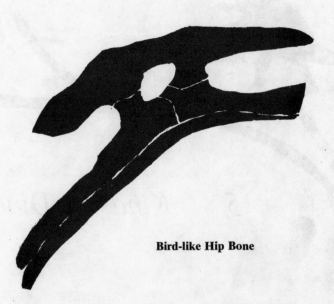

Bird-like Hip Bone

46

Both groups of dinosaurs began as small, two-legged reptiles. They were swift, meat-eating hunters. Most dinosaurs in both groups grew larger. Their eating habits changed over the years and many of them became four-legged.

The saurischian dinosaurs, those with lizard-like hip bones, were further divided into two groups. The theropods (THEER-uh-podds) were the flesh-eating giants like **Allosaurus** (al-luh-SAWR-us) and **Tyrannosaurus.** They were the only dinosaurs that remained pretty much like their thecodont ancestors—two-legged, active, meat eaters.

The sauropods (SAWR-uh-podds) were the giant, swampland plant-eaters like **Brontosaurus** (bront-uh-SAWR-us), **Diplodocus** (dih-PLODD-uh-kuss) and **Brachiosaurus** (BRAKE-e-uh-SAWR-us). They were huge creatures and spent most of their time in shallow waters that helped support heavy bodies. They had no reason to keep the two-legged posture that was good for running after game. The sauropods came down on all fours.

Lizard-like Hip Bone

47

The ornithischian dinosaurs, with bird-like hip bones, were divided into four groups. There were the ornithopods (OR-nith-uh-PODDS) which were duck-billed. Stegosaurs (STEGG-uh-sawrs) and ankylosaurs (ANG-kull-uh-SAWRS) were armored. The ceratopsians (serr-uh-TOPS-e-yunns) were horned. They were all plant-eaters and usually four-legged.

Careful study of fossils bones proves that although some kinds of dinosaurs may look alike, they come from different groups.

Let's check on a few points. First, we know how scientists divide the 140 million years of the Age of Reptiles into periods. It is hard to remember scientific names, but if we try to use too many every-day names we might become confused.

The Age of Reptiles is called the Mesozoic Era. Each era is divided into periods. The three periods of the Mesozoic Era are: Triassic (try-ASS-ick), Jurassic (joo-RASS-ick) and Cretaceous (kree-TAY-shuss).

The first and oldest period, Triassic, began about 200 million years ago. It was then the first dinosaurs appeared on earth. The last and youngest period, Cretaceous, ended about 60 million years ago. If we wanted to use everyday names, we could call these 140 millions of years the Age of Reptiles. And we could name the periods First, Middle, and Last.

Many people call the flying reptiles and sea reptiles dinosaurs, too, because they lived at the same time. The flying reptiles, or pterosaurs, did come from the same thecodont ancestors as the two groups of dinosaurs. But the sea reptiles did not. The picture chart on page 49 explains this. We will talk about these reptiles in separate chapters.

MESOZOIC ERA
(mess-uh-ZO-ick)

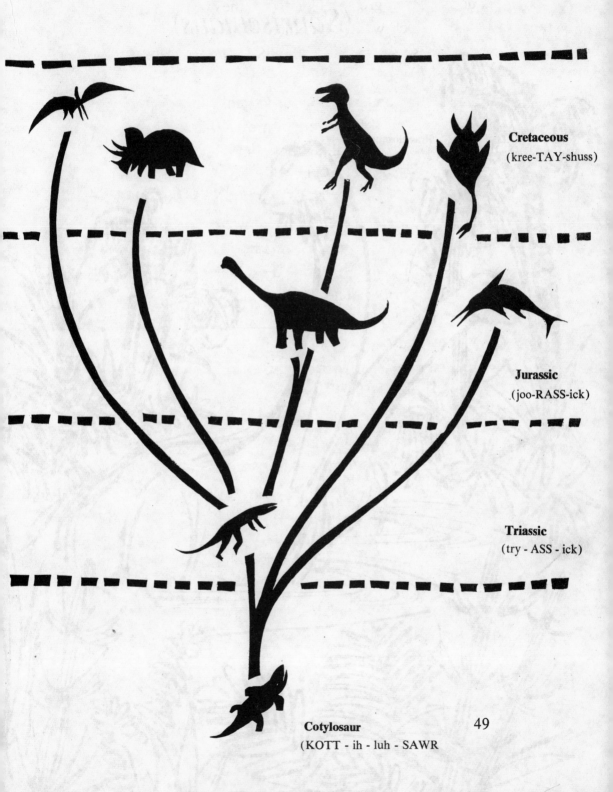

Cretaceous
(kree-TAY-shuss)

Jurassic
(joo-RASS-ick)

Triassic
(try - ASS - ick)

Cotylosaur
(KOTT - ih - luh - SAWR

49

6   *Lizard-Hipped Dinosaurs (Saurischians)*

Brachiosaurus

The saurischian (sawr-ISS-kee-yunn) dinosaurs all had lizard-like hip bones. You know that there are two separate groups of saurischians. One group is the theropods, and the other is the sauropods.

These two types of dinosaurs did not look very much alike nor did they act very much alike. The theropods were flesh-eaters and the sauropods were plant-eaters.

6.1 Theropods

All of the theropods were two-legged and meat-eaters. Of all the dinosaurs, the theropods were the most like their thecodont ancestors.

As we look at the different kinds of dinosaurs we see that all dinosaurs, except the theropods, became plant-eaters. Most of the plant-eaters were creatures that came down on all four legs. But all of the known flesh-eating theropods, from the earliest Triassic forms to the latest Cretaceous forms, walked on two legs.

We also notice that the theropods lived and developed from the beginning to the very end of the Age of Reptiles. This is unusual. The other kinds of dinosaurs lived for a certain time on earth, then disappeared as other forms took their place. The flesh-eating theropods were probably the most successful of all dinosaurs. They survived in the changing environment over the millions of years that dinosaurs ruled the earth.

Theropods were hunters. Their food was other animals. The theropods grew in size feeding on the plant-eaters. So, we find that most theropods of late Cretaceous times were bigger than the early flesh-eaters.

Probably the best known theropod is **Tyrannosaurus rex.** He was the king of the flesh-eaters in Cretaceous days. But there were also other flesh-eaters roaming the forests and sand bars with the "tyrant lizard king." Some were almost as large, and some were much smaller. They all looked very much alike, however.

6.11 **Megalosaurus**

Megalosaurus (MEGG-uh-luh-SAWR-us) is the name given to the remains of giant flesh-eating dinosaurs that lived in Jurassic days. **Megalosaurus** moved swiftly on two strong hind legs. The small forearms were provided with three sharp claws.

6.12 **Ornitholestes**

Ornitholestes (OR-nith-uh-LESS-teez) was a small flesh-eater that lived some 155 to 120 million years ago in the Jurassic period. From head to tail it measured about five or six feet. That is as long as a man is tall. But part of its length was in the tail that dragged behind. The tail helped balance its body.

52

You can see how this worked if you try to balance a long pencil on your finger. You know that if one side is longer than the other, the weight of the longer side pulls it down.

The flesh-eaters did not walk upright like human beings. The front part of their bodies leaned forward in order to balance their weight over the hips. They needed long heavy tails to help keep their heads up.

Ornitholestes was a very light and graceful dinosaur. Its bird-like hind legs were very strong. It probably darted swiftly in and out of the forest greenery in search of prey.

Like all flesh-eaters, it had small arms. They ended in long, grasping "fingers."

Ornitholestes preyed upon the small reptiles that lived in rock crannies or climbed the stems of ferns. Its head was small and light and the mouth was armed with sharp teeth for biting and tearing flesh. The dinosaur was a hunter of small game.

Ornitholestes

53

6.13 Allosaurus

Living at the same time as **Ornitholestes** was the giant **Allosaurus** (al-luh-SAWR-us). **Allosaurus** means "other lizard." He looked and acted so much like the smaller flesh-eater that you might think he was just a grown-up **Ornitholestes. Allosaurus** was a two-legged flesh-eater.

An animal cannot just grow larger and larger. If a giant animal is to survive, the body and skeleton must change and become stronger to support the greater weight. **Allosaurus** had big and strong hind legs to hold up his heavy body. He was about thirty-five feet long and fourteen feet tall. His tail made up more than one half of his length. This frightening monster could easily have peeked into a second-floor window if there had been any houses then.

He had short arms and his hands were armed with sharp, hook-like claws. Powerful three-toed hind feet, also clawed, could pin his victim to the ground.

Allosaurus had a huge head about the size of the scoop on a steam-shovel. Three-foot jaws were lined with dagger-like teeth. One great bite could tear the flesh from the bones of his victims.

Few animals that he attacked could get away from those powerful jaws and sharp claws. His head was large but not heavy. The skull had openings in the bone to make it lighter in weight.

Allosaurus was the terrible monster of Jurassic days. He was the hunter of big game. When **Allosaurus** ran out of the forest, every other creature scurried for safety.

We know that **Allosaurus** killed and ate the giant plant-eaters. The proof came from Wyoming. A **Brontosaurus** skeleton was found with tooth marks on many of the bones and parts of the backbone missing. An **Allosaurus** jaw was compared with these tooth marks, and they matched perfectly. Broken teeth of **Allosaurus** and the bones of **Brontosaurus** were found together.

Allosaurus

Allosaurus moved quickly, on hind legs that were built for speed. There were probably many fierce battles between these great flesh-eaters and their victims. But **Allosaurus** lived during a time when most of the plant-eaters had little means of protecting themselves.

Allosaurus was a mighty king but his reign came to an end. The great theropod gave way to a still larger and fiercer form of dinosaur that ruled through Cretaceous days until the Age of Reptiles came to an end.

The American Museum of Natural History in New York City has a skeleton of **Allosaurus** mounted as though this mighty hunter were feeding on a dead **Brontosaurus.** Also, a skull of **Allosaurus** may be seen in the Denver Museum of Natural History.

6.14 Tyrannosaurus rex

One of the meanest and most terrible monsters that ever lived was **Tyrannosaurus rex** (tih-RAN-uh-SAWR-us rex) the King of Tyrants. He lived some 120 to 60 million years ago in Cretaceous days, the last period of the Age of Reptiles. **Allosaurus** was gone. Other flesh-eaters like the smaller **Gorgosaurus** (gor-guh-SAWR-us) stalked game in the thick forests. But **Tyrannosaurus** was the most frightening creature on land.

Standing on his two strong hind legs, this monster was twenty feet tall. That is taller than a two-story house. **Tyrannosaurus** was almost fifty feet long from the tip of his nose to the tip of his tail, and weighed about ten tons.

Changes took place in **Tyrannosaurus'** body and skeleton just as with **Allosaurus.** The legs and hip bones grew very big and strong. A man 6 feet tall would only reach up to **Tyrannosaurus'** knee.

56

The front "arms" seem too tiny for such a fierce and huge monster. **Tyrannosaurus** did not use his arms so much as did **Allosaurus.** The arms became smaller—about the size of a man's arm. But they had two hooked claws with a grip of iron.

The head was tremendous—more than four feet long. The mouth opened a yard wide. This frightening creature could have swallowed a creature as large as a man in one gulp. The double-edged teeth could be up to six inches long, and like **Allosaurus',** as sharp as daggers.

Tyrannosaurus stalked his game along the shores of rivers and lakes. Here were the great trachodonts that fed on trailing water plants and soft bulbs along the shore. **Tyrannosaurus** would eat any animal, but he preferred the largest ones. He needed tons of flesh for a single meal.

Tyrannosaurus rex

We can see **Tyrannosaurus** moving quickly on his hind legs as he darts from the trees at the edge of the forest. A peaceful plant-eater, quietly feeding along the lakeshore, tries to escape the hungry flesh-eater. But **Tyrannosaurus** leaps and holds his victim. Soon the struggle is over. **Tyrannosaurus** is still king—he begins to eat his dinner.

His teeth tear out hundred-pound chunks of flesh which he swallows whole. With his meal finished, he returns to the forest to sleep. When he is hungry, he will awaken to hunt more food. But the King of Tyrants rules his kingdom unmolested.

Tyrannosaurus had no enemies except, perhaps, another **Tyrannosaurus** who fought with him over a meal. The great reptile was perfectly built for the part he played in dinosaur history—the king of flesh-eaters. But when the end of the dinosaurs came, **Tyrannosaurus** disappeared with all the others.

A skeleton of **Tyrannosaurus** is on display in the American Museum of Natural History in New York City.

6.15 Struthiomimus

Struthiomimus (STROOTH-ee-uh-MIME-us) was a different kind of theropod. He belonged to the family of flesh-eaters. But for some reason he began to eat fruits, green plants and insects, besides small reptiles—as some birds do today. In fact, he looked so much like a bird-reptile that he is often called the "ostrich dinosaur."

This medium-sized reptile walked and ran on two hind legs like the other theropods. But his legs were not so thick and strong. They were long and thin—more like a big bird's. But he could run very fast. To balance his body he had the long tail of the flesh-eater. Like **Ornitholestes,** he had long-fingered, grasping hands.

His head and neck were different from most dinosaurs. The neck was long and ostrich-like and ended in a very small head. The mouth had no teeth. The flat horny beak also resembled the ostrich's.

Struthiomimus was a harmless creature. He appeared at the end of the reign of dinosaurs and his years on earth were short.

Struthiomimus

6.2 Sauropods

The plant-eating sauropods were the largest land animals that ever lived. The only animals that have grown bigger than dinosaurs are whales. Water helps hold up the huge body of a whale. Some whales are longer than the longest dinosaurs and three times as heavy.

Big bodies and small brains were very much in fashion during Jurassic times. But the giant sauropods were harmless creatures in spite of their great size.

The earth helped these dinosaurs to grow into such huge creatures. The climate was tropical. Many lakes, marshes, and swamps grew thick with soft, bulbous water plants. For hundreds and thousands of generations, the dinosaurs that lived in and near the swamplands found food plentiful and their bodies enabled them to get along in that kind of world.

6.21 Plateosaurus

Plateosaurus (PLATT-ee-uh-SAWR-us) was one of the first giant plant-eaters. It was 20 feet in length. It had a long tail and a fairly long neck topped with a small head.

Plateosaurus shows how the plant-eaters began to change from their ancestors, the thecodont flesh-eaters. A medium-sized dinosaur, it tramped across the Triassic lowlands on its strong hind legs just like its thecodont and theropod cousins. But the front arms of **Plateosaurus** had grown large. The front arms were bigger because **Plateosaurus** used them in coming down on all four legs to feed. We will see how the later sauropods changed to a completely four-footed posture.

Another change was taking place in **Plateosaurus.** This was in the teeth. All the flesh-eating dinosaurs had long sharp teeth for tearing flesh. **Plateosaurus'** teeth were not sharp blades like a flesh-eater's. They were flatter and the tips were quite blunt. Teeth of this kind were better for the chopping and cutting of leafy, green plants.

Plateosaurus

Plateosaurus is a good example of an in-between dinosaur. It had many of the habits of the flesh-eaters. Yet it showed the beginnings of habits that were to develop into the strictly plant-eating dinosaur.

6.22 Brontosaurus

Brontosaurus (bront-uh-SAWR-us) is the best-known of the Jurassic swampland dinosaurs. When most people think of dinosaurs, they think of **Brontosaurus.** Most of the giant Jurassic plant-eaters resembled this dinosaur that roamed the earth some 155 to 120 million years ago.

It is difficult to imagine the great size of **Brontosaurus.** The dinosaur stood about 15 feet high and was very long—70 or 80 feet from nose to tail tip. The whiplike tail was the longest part of the creature. Its bulging 35 ton body was held up by four legs that looked like tree stumps.

Brontosaurus was bigger than any animal you have ever seen and weighed more than a whole family of elephants. An elephant looks huge to us. It is the largest land animal alive today. But beside a **Brontosaurus,** an Indian elephant weighing five tons would look like a mouse.

The name **Brontosaurus** means "thunder lizard." The man who named it thought that the earth must have thundered under the weight of the animal, as it plodded across the land.

The hind legs were longer and stronger than the front ones. The feet were broad and short, and they had curved claws—three on each of the hind legs, and one on each of the front legs.

Some scientists once thought that **Brontosaurus** could walk only in water which would help hold up the huge body. But tracks were found in Texas where a number of these dinosaurs had crossed a sandbar, probably from one lagoon to another. The fossil tracks were deep. They showed that each dinosaur's full weight was on its legs and that no water held up the body.

It is true that the four tree-like legs were not much good for walking on dry land. Such legs were better for feeding slowly along the shores of lakes and swamps where **Brontosaurus** spent most of its life. Sometimes the dinosaurs floated in deeper water.

The head of **Brontosaurus** was so tiny that it must have looked funny on such a huge creature. The brain was so small for the size of the body that this dinosaur must have been the most stupid animal that ever lived. **Brontosaurus** was certainly not a "thinking" animal. It knew enough to eat, sleep, lay eggs, and move away from an enemy. This was instinct (or un-learned behavior), and it knew little else.

The mouth seemed like a slit at the end of a 20 foot neck. **Brontosaurus** probably had to eat almost all the time. It had to get enough food through its tiny mouth to keep the great body alive. A five-ton elephant eats about 100 to 200 pounds of green fodder and 20 pounds of grain every day. Cold-blooded reptiles do not need as much food as warm-blooded animals, but it is quite possible that **Brontosaurus** ate at least 1000 pounds of green leaves or plants each day.

Its teeth were very weak. **Brontosaurus** nibbled or tore off soft, juicy swamp plants which were swallowed whole. Some scientists think that these teeth were only choppers and that the huge plant-eaters had to depend upon gizzard stones, or gastroliths, to help grind up their food.

Birds, like chickens or canaries, peck at gravel. It goes into their gizzards and helps grind up their food. Birds are descended from reptiles.

Polished gastroliths have been found inside dinosaur skeletons between the ribs where the gizzard might have been. These shiny, smooth, round stones are found only in dinosaur fossil country. Dinosaur hunters near the Colorado-Utah border have found many of these gastroliths. In fact, you can buy them at the Dinosaur National Monument, Vernal, Utah.

It is possible that the idea about the dinosaurs' gizzard stones is true, but it has not been proved. It cannot be accepted as a scientific

Plateosaurus

Cotylosaur

Triassic

Allosaurus

Stegosaurus

Jurassic

Brontosaurus

Ornitholestes

Tyrannosaurus rex

Corythosaurus

Ankylosaur

Cretaceous

fact until someone finds a petrified dinosaur gizzard with the stones in it.

Brontosaurus did not spend much time on dry land. The creature had to come onto dry land to lay eggs or perhaps to cross a sandbar to find a new lagoon. **Brontosaurus** moved too slowly on land to escape the swift **Allosaurus.**

You can see the finest mounted skeleton of a **Brontosaurus** at the American Museum of Natural History in New York City.

Brontosaurus

6.23 Diplodocus

Diplodocus (dih-PLODD-uh-kuss) was another giant plant-eater that lived in Jurassic days. The name means "double beam" and was given to this dinosaur because of the double spines along the backbone. It was about 80 feet long and looked like **Brontosaurus.** But **Diplodocus'** 25-ton body was narrower and the neck and tail were longer.

The head was even smaller than that of **Brontosaurus.** The teeth were weak pegs, no bigger around than lead pencils. With these, **Diplodocus** probably chopped off about 1000 pounds of plants and leaves every day. Its nostrils were on top of the head so the animal could breathe while its body was under water. **Diplodocus** lived a quiet life in the soggy swamplands. The finest skeletons of **Diplodocus** may be seen in the Denver Museum of Natural History and the Carnegie Museum in Pittsburgh, Pennsylvania.

6.24 Brachiosaurus

The biggest of all the sauropods was **Brachiosaurus** (BRAKE-e-uh-SAWR-us). It was not so long as **Brontosaurus** or **Diplodocus,** but its body was much heavier.

This giant plant-eater was different from the other two giants. The front legs of **Brachiosaurus** were larger than the hind legs. Its neck was very long and heavy, and the tail just barely touched the ground. With the taller front legs, **Brachiosaurus** did not need a long tail for a balance. The shoulders were almost 18 feet above the ground.

Brachiosaurus was about 45 feet tall. Its nostrils were on a hump on top of the head. The animal waded on four great legs along the bottom of fairly deep water where it was able to poke its head above the surface to breathe and look around.

Everything about **Brachiosaurus** was big except the head. The brain was small and practically useless. When danger came near, its only defense was to lumber into 40 feet of water. There it could pop up its head, periscope-like, to watch the jaws of **Allo-saurus** clamp down on some other victim.

7 Bird-like Hipped Dinosaurs (*Ornithischians*)

Scientists say that ornithischian (or-nih-THISK-e-yunn) dinosaurs, with bird-like hip bones, changed greatly during Cretaceous times.

Stegosaurus

By the end of the Jurassic days the giants, like **Brontosaurus** and **Brachiosaurus,** had disappeared and new kinds of dinosaur plant-eaters had begun to appear. These new ornithischian dinosaurs developed into some of the strangest forms of all. Strange and weird as they may seem to us, there were good reasons for their being so.

Allosaurus

The earth had changed by the end of the Cretaceous period and the last dinosaurs were different from the early ones.

Ornithischian dinosaurs were adapted to their environment. For one thing, they could feed well on the changing vegetable food supply. The great swamps of Jurassic days with vast supplies of tender water-plants were slowly disappearing as the earth gradually pushed upward.

New foods meant newer kinds of teeth and jaws for biting and chewing them. Eating habits changed. Along with the changed eating habits, dinosaurs' bodies changed in other ways.

The greatest changes in ornithischian dinosaurs were their ways of protecting themselves. The most spectacular plant-eaters of Jurassic days stayed in the water most of the time and this gave them some protection from the flesh-eaters. But in Cretaceous days, more and more of the plant-eating dinosaurs moved onto the land.

With the mighty King of Tyrants and others like him stalking the forests, the land plant-eaters had to develop other ways to defend themselves. Some, like **Trachodon,** took to the deep water. Others, like **Paleoscincus** (PAY-lee-uh-SKINK-us), developed plates of armor. Still others, like **Triceratops** (try-SERR-uh-topps) developed sharp points and horns that were handy in parrying the attacks of the hungry flesh-eaters.

Let's look at the most spectacular forms of ornithischian dinosaurs. There were many bird-hipped dinosaurs. The uplands and lake shores were filled with many different kinds.

The ornithischian dinosaurs are divided into four groups—the ornithopods (OR-nith-uh-PODDS), the stegosaurs (STEGG-uh-sawrs), the ankylosaurs (ANG-kull-uh-SAWRS), and the cera-topsians (serr-uh-TOPS-e-yunns). We will look at several kinds of dinosaurs in each group.

7.1 Ornithopods

Ornithopods, the first group of the bird-hipped dinosaurs, show the least number of changes. The word ornithopod means "bird-like feet." The "duck-billed" dinosaurs were ornithopods with webbed duck-like feet. They were all plant-eaters.

7.11 Camptosaurus

Camptosaurus (kamp-tuh-SAWR-us) was one of the first of the ornithischian dinosaurs. It lived about 120 million years ago in late Jurassic and early Cretaceous times. The animal was about five to eight feet long.

Camptosaurus and its close relatives first appeared about 140 million years ago. This was toward the end of the Jurassic period. They lived on into the early Cretaceous times. Usually, these plant-eating dinosaurs walked on two legs. They could come down on all fours, and probably did so quite often. Their front legs were not good for walking. They were used for swimming and for pushing themselves upright after feeding on low ground plants.

The skull of **Camptosaurus** was low and long. It had no teeth in the front of the mouth. This is true of almost all ornithischian dinosaurs. The front of the jaws formed a bird-like beak. When the animal was alive, the beak was probably covered with a horny sheath that was good for biting and cutting plant food. Along the sides of the jaws there were rows of flat, knife-like teeth that could cut and chew the green plants.

Camptosaurus

Each new kind of dinosaur began as a rather simple form. We find that the camptosaurs were the first simple form of the ornithischian dinosaurs. From them came the **Trachodon** (TRACK-uh-donn) and the thick-skulled **Troödon** (TRO-uh-donn). Camptosaurs were the ancestors of the many different kinds of armored and horned dinosaurs.

In some of the later forms, we still see the camptosaur-like mouth with the bird-like beak, even though the bodies have changed into some weird forms.

72

7.12 Iguanodon

The first dinosaur ever to be described was the **Iguanodon** (ih-GWANN-uh-dunn). In 1822, Dr. Gideon Mantell found the fossilized teeth and skeleton of an ancient reptile which he named **Iguanodon.** The story of his discovery is told in the chapter on Early Dinosaur Hunters.

Dr. Mantell knew about the living South American iguanas. These reptiles live on the Galapagos Islands off the coast of Chile. They eat seaweed and swim far from shore to feed.

An iguana swims like a crocodile with its legs pressed close to its sides. Its body and sweeping tail move through the water like a snake. It is probably the way **Iguanodon** swam. Although this dinosaur is not related to the iguanas living today, it looked so much like them that Dr. Mantell named the first dinosaur skeleton ever discovered after them.

Iguanodon fossils are found in early Cretaceous rocks. These plant-eating dinosaurs are closely related to **Camptosaurus.**

Both dinosaurs spent some time in the water. When they came on land, they usually walked on two legs, somewhat like the flesh-eaters. But **Iguanodon** could also come down on all four legs to nibble ground plants. The front legs were small and not good for walking. In fact, both dinosaurs resembled kangaroos.

Iguanodon's mouth was similar to **Camptosaurus'.** It was a horny beak with no teeth in front. The teeth were lined in rows along the sides of the mouth. With its beak, **Iguanodon** cut green plants from stems and then chewed with the teeth further back in the mouth.

Many skeletons of **Iguanodon** have been found in Europe, but we have none in North American museums. Seventeen skeletons

Iguanodon

74

were found in a coal mine at Bernissart, Belgium. Scientists say that during the great earth changes in the Cretaceous period, a swift river cut its way through the rocks. The new river cut a canyon about 750 feet deep.

Then earth conditions changed again and the river became a slow-moving stream with marshy banks. The deep canyon began to fill with sediments. Along the shores of this stream the **Iguanodon** lived in the thick vegetation. When they died their skeletons were covered over and became fossilized. They lay untouched for about 70 million years until Belgian coal miners dug into the rock. Now, these fossils can be seen in a museum in Brussels, Belgium.

In the peat beds of western Colorado, scientists have found what are believed to be thirty-four-inch-long footprints of **Iguanodon.** If these really are the footprints of **Iguanodon,** it is a great mystery why no bones of these animals have been found in North America.

7.13 Trachodon

Trachodon (TRACK-uh-donn), or **Hadrosaurus** (had-ruh-SAWR-us) has the common name "duck-bill" because of the shape of its jaws.

These duck-billed dinosaurs lived along the lake shores and rivers in late Cretaceous days, about 60 million years ago. Harmless plant-eaters, they shared the water-plants and mollusks of the banks or strands with their crested cousins **Saurolophus** (sawr-AHL-uh-fuss), **Corythosaurus** (KOR-ith-uh-SAWR-us), and **Parasaurolophus** (PAR-uh-sawr-AH-luh-fuss). All of these dinosaurs were water-lovers.

Saurolophus

The climate of the northern part of North America where the duck-bills lived was much warmer at the end of the Cretaceous period than it is now. Scientists have found evidence of many warm-climate trees and plants along with the skeletons of **Trachodon** and other duck-billed dinosaurs.

Thick forests of ginkgos, palm and fig trees, and even redwood trees, like those living today along the California coast, covered the uplands. Bordering the lakes and rivers were vast areas of water plants. **Trachodon** and his cousins must have eaten great quantities of these plants.

Trachodon

77

Trachodon, or Hadrosaurus, is the most typical kind of duck-billed dinosaur. The body and habits of Trachodon give us a good idea of most of the duck-bills. You may remember in the chapter on Early Dinosaur Hunters that the first dinosaur skeleton discovered in North America was a Hadrosaurus. You will find some museums that have a mounted skeleton named Hadrosaurus. Other museums have mounted skeletons named Trachodon. They are both similar duck-billed dinosaurs. We will describe and talk of Trachodon. However, the description will also fit Hadrosaurus.

If you compare the pictures, or skeletons, a glance will show that Trachodon looked like a Camptosaurus grown large. But Trachodon's skull was more flattened, especially in the front, to form the broad duck-bill. This plant-eater also walked on two hind legs. But it could come down on all fours, as did Camptosaurus.

Trachodon was about 30 feet long and stood 16 feet high. It was big but, of course, not so large as Brontosaurus. Shaped something like a big kangaroo, Trachodon had short arms, long hind legs, and a wide, thick tail.

It is believed that the duck-bills dredged in the mud or sand of the lake shores for any tidbits they could find there. But the teeth show that Trachodon fed mostly on soft plants.

Trachodon had no teeth in the front of the bill. But on each side of both jaws, above and below, there were about 500 teeth. So, a duck-billed dinosaur may have had 2000 teeth, or more, in his mouth! The small, cough-drop shaped teeth were arranged in closely packed rows, practically one row on top of the next. As the

Plant-eater's Teeth

teeth began to wear off, the overlapping surfaces formed a rough pavement that ground the food, like a mill grinds grain, into a pulpy mass.

It seems that **Trachodon** had a steady supply of new teeth. As each old tooth wore off, a new tooth pushed up from underneath to replace it. So, the duck-bills were equipped with a very efficient mouth-machine for biting and chewing their food.

For a long time, scientists guessed about the kind of skin **Trachodon** wore. The big, harmless plant-eater had no way of protecting itself that could be seen. Did **Trachodon** have a thick, tough skin, or perhaps a scaly one? Some living animals, like the elephant or rhinoceros, have very thick skins that give them some protection.

No one could answer this question until a man named Charles H. Sternberg of Kansas found a duck-bill "mummy" in 1908. The dried-up dinosaur, probably 60 to 70 million years old, showed exactly what **Trachodon's** skin was like. It was thin, pebbled skin, like the covering on a golf ball. There were no scales or any other kind of protective armor. What color the skin was there is no way of telling. But we know it was lighter on the under side of the body than on the back.

The duck-bill mummy had died a natural death. The **Trachodon** found in Kansas was probably washed up on a wide sand flat. There it lay undisturbed for some time while the hot sun dried up the soft insides and muscles. The leg skin shrank and became hard and leathery. As the flesh dried, the skin over the stomach sank into the body cavity and gathered into folds and creases along the animal's sides.

79

We suppose that the water-level rose and the dried body was covered quickly with fine river sand. Before the dried skin had a chance to soften in the water, enough clay in the river sand made a perfect impression of the tiny knobs on the skin. Now scientists can see, with a magnifying glass, every detail of the skin as it once was, even though the skin itself disappeared millions of years ago.

Almost everything about **Trachodon** shows that it spent most of its time in or near the water. It probably swam very much like **Iguanodon** or the living South American iguanas. **Trachodon** was probably a fine swimmer. The tremendous plant-eaters like **Brontosaurus** also spent much time in the water, but they were not swimmers.

Proof of **Trachodon's** walking and swimming habits are found in the preserved mummies. The hind feet were three-toed. It had

Corythosaurus

Lambeosaurus

small arms and hands that ended in fingers which were connected by skin. They formed paddles like the webbed feet of a duck. **Trachodon** would have had little use for webbed feet if it had not spent much time in the water.

The ability to swim swiftly was **Trachodon's** only means of protection against flesh-eaters. The duck-bills came out on land to lay eggs and to feed, but otherwise seldom ventured far from water. They probably varied their vegetable diet with fresh-water clams or mussels.

Trachodon had many interesting relatives. They all lived very much like this duck-bill. Some of them developed very strange-looking crests on their heads. Scientists say that the crest may have been an air-storage chamber that helped the animal to stay under water for longer periods of time.

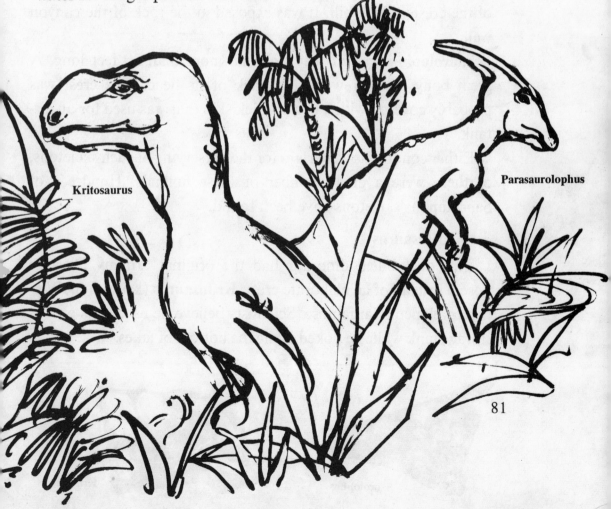

Kritosaurus

Parasaurolophus

81

7.14 Saurolophus

Saurolophus (sawr-AHL-uh-fuss), a crested dinosaur, was discovered by Dr. Barnum Brown in the Red Deer River area of Alberta, Canada. This area has yielded many fine specimens of crested dinosaurs. The skeleton had pieces of skin clinging to it. The sandstone, in which it was found, showed water ripples and the imprints of horsetail rushes.

The animal probably was buried in much the same way as was the fossilized "mummy" of **Trachodon.** Fine sand settled over the bones. Million of years later the fine sand had become sandstone and the bones were petrified. With the uplift of the earth in that region, a new river cut a deep gorge down through the rocks.

More millions of years later, Dr. Brown discovered the bones of the crested duck-bill. It was exposed in the rock of the canyon wall.

Saurolophus was 17 feet high and more than 30 feet long. A great bony crest grew on the back of its head. The crest was probably covered with a bag of thick skin that was used for an air-tank.

Either conditions were right for the preserving of such skeletons, or there were a great number of these animals. Hundreds of **Saurolophus** skeletons have been found.

7.15 Kritosaurus

This duck-billed dinosaur had the original "Jimmy Durante nose." Instead of an elaborate crest, **Kritosaurus** (kritt-uh-SAWR-us) developed a large nose. Scientists believe he used it as an air-storage tank while he poked along the bottom of lakes.

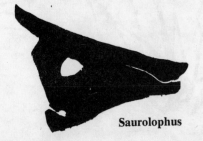

Saurolophus

Kritosaurus

7.16 Corythosaurus

Another crested dinosaur was found by Dr. Brown in the Red Deer River gorge. It was named **Corythosaurus** (KOR-ith-uh-SAWR-us) which, in a kind of Greek shorthand, means "Corinthian-helmeted reptile." Indeed, its head does look like the helmet of an ancient Greek warrior. The fossil shows the grainy imprints of the skin and some of the tendons of the animal.

Many **Unio** shells were found close to the skeleton. The **Unio** is a fresh water clam that is no longer found in the Western Hemisphere. **Corythosaurus** was 18 feet long and, like **Trachodon,** a good swimmer.

7.17 Lambeosaurus

Lambeosaurus (LAMB-e-uh-SAWR-us) was another first cousin to **Trachodon.** Its air-storage crest was shaped somewhat like a double hatchet.

7.18 Parasaurolophus

Parasaurolophus (PAR-uh-sawr-AH-luh-fuss) had a horn-like crest. It extended far back beyond its head like a long plume. The long crest makes us think of a goat. The crest was really a long nasal passage. It probably worked like an air-tank to help the duck-bill stay under water.

Parasaurolophus

7.19 Troödon

There is a group of ornithopod dinosaurs that are well-known for their thick, bone skulls. One of the earliest forms of the bone-headed dinosaurs was **Troödon** (TRO-uh-donn) which appeared 120 million years ago. **Troödon** was smaller than most ornithopods. It was only about 6 feet long. The head was quite strange.

Troödon

83

Corythosaurus

Lambeosaurus

It developed a dome-shaped roof over the brain—a ceiling of solid bone. On the nose and at the back of the neck there were fearsome nodes, spikes, and points.

7.191 Pachycephalosaurus

Pachycephalosaurus (pack-uh-SEFF-uh-luh-SAWR-us), a late Cretaceous relative of **Troödon,** also had a dome-shaped bone roof over its brain. But this bone was about ten inches thick. It is a mystery why the tiny brain of this dinosaur needed such a tremendous bone protection.

7.2 Stegosaurs

The second group of dinosaurs with bird-like hips is the stegosaurs. Big plant-eaters, like **Trachodon,** protected themselves from the flesh-eaters by escaping into deep water. But plant-eaters that spent more time on land developed coats of armor for protection. Some of these armored dinosaurs had bony clubs or spikes at the ends of their tails. The tails were good weapons for fighting off attacking meat-eaters.

7.21 Stegosaurus

Stegosaurus (stegg-uh-SAWR-us) was an armored dinosaur. He lived in the last part of the Jurassic period, more than 120 million years ago. His body was about 20 feet long. He carried his tiny head rather close to the ground as he poked about eating ground plants. Four thick legs with padded feet held up his heavy body. The front legs were only knee-high to the back ones, so he stood about 10 feet high over the hips.

Two alternate rows of almost heart-shaped plates ran along the middle of his back from head to tail. The plates above the hips

84

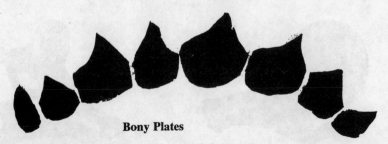

Bony Plates

were about two feet high. They were not more than an inch thick and may have been covered with a horny layer when **Stegosaurus** was alive. They probably discouraged many an **Allosaurus** that sprang on his back and got a mouthful of the sharp-edged blades.

Four huge spikes, close to three feet long and from three to six inches wide at the base, grew at the tip of the tail. When **Stegosaurus** swung this weapon around it must have swept everything from his path.

The tiny head was hardly more than a bump at the end of his body. He moved slowly chopping off plants with his horny beak.

Stegosaurus had one of the smallest brains for his size of any backboned land animal. His body was bigger than an elephant, but his brain was hardly the size of a kitten's. A nerve center in the hips grew 20 times the size of the brain.

Some people believe **Stegosaurus** had two brains, one in the tail and one in the head. This is not true. But many jokes were made about it, such as: The stegosaur had great intellectual length; that he could make both head and tail of any problem; that he always had an afterthought. The nerve center in his hips did control the movements of his tail and hind legs, but it was not a brain. Truly, **Stegosaurus** must have been even more stupid than **Brontosaurus.**

Ankylosaurus

7.3 Ankylosaurs

The third group of ornithischian dinosaurs is the ankylosaurs. The ankylosaurs were really armor-plated all over. Head, body, and tail were covered with overlapping bony plates, like the armadillo.

7.31 Ankylosaurus

Ankylosaurus (ANG-kull-uh-SAWR-us), the armor-covered dinosaur, lived in the Cretaceous period. His low, squat body was protected by heavy bone plates. Even the head was plated. The heavy, stiff tail ended in a huge club-like mass of bone.

Nibbling plants and minding his own business, he lumbered along on his short legs. If some hungry flesh-eater was silly enough to try to make a meal of **Ankylosaurus,** the armored dinosaur merely swung his tail club and dealt a crushing blow. He was fairly safe within his shell.

Most of the other armored dinosaurs of Cretaceous days looked very much like **Ankylosaurus.**

Nodosaurus (no-duh-SAWR-us) may have rolled up into a ball as an armadillo does when attacked. **Paleoscincus** (PAY-lee-uh-SKINK-us) was armored from head to tail with a row of sharp spikes sticking out along the lower sides of his body. Even **Tyrannosaurus** must have steered clear of him.

86

7.4 Ceratopsians

The fourth group of dinosaurs with bird-like hip bones is the ceratopsians, or horned dinosaurs. They were the last to appear, and lived only during the Cretaceous period, about 120 to 60 million years ago.

All of the ceratopsians were plant-eating land animals. They lived in the marshlands of the great inland sea area, east of the Rocky Mountains. Some very fine fossils of ceratopsians have been found in Alberta, Canada and in the Gobi Desert.

They wandered through high grass and among palm, fig, and redwood trees. The big horned dinosaurs could protect themselves well against the flesh-eating hunters. They could charge forward and perhaps frighten even a hungry **Tyrannosaurus.**

7.41 Psittacosaurus

Scientists say that the small **Psittacosaurus** (SIT-uh-kuh-SAWR-us) that ran about on its hind legs was probably an ancestor of the ceratopsians. It lived in the first part of the Cretaceous period. The narrow head ended in a large parrot-like beak from which it was named "parrot lizard." It was not so strange or fierce looking as the ceratopsians that came later.

Psittacosaurus

7.42 Protoceratops

Protoceratops (pro-toh-SERR-uh-tops) was the first of the frilled ceratopsians. Its fossil eggs and skeletons found together in the Gobi Desert proved to scientists that dinosaurs did lay eggs. The eggs were 6 to 8 inches long.

Six or eight feet in length, **Protoceratops** walked on all four bowed legs. Its head was large. The front of the mouth formed a sharp, hooked beak. The back of the skull frilled out like a great collar covering the neck and shoulders. **Protoceratops** had no teeth in the front of its jaws. But there were two useless, tiny teeth on each side of its mouth.

88

The American Museum of Natural History expedition that found dinosaurs eggs in the Gobi Desert also found a number of skulls. From these skulls scientists learned how **Protoceratops** grew from the newly hatched baby to the full grown adult.

Protoceratops had only a very small hump on his nose which was the beginning of a horn. But the giant horned dinosaurs of the last part of the Cretaceous period developed from this fat-tailed creature.

7.43 Triceratops

A drawing of **Triceratops** (try-SERR-uh-tops) shows us how much he resembles the rhinoceros. **Triceratops** was a plant-eater. He was about 30 feet long and probably weighed ten tons. His chunky body was some eight feet high at the hips. The short, stocky legs ended in broad hoofed feet.

Tyrannosaurus rex

A huge head accounted for a third of his full length. The skull was about eight feet long. Half of this was the great frill or shield that covered the neck and shoulders like a hood. The front of his head was narrow and ended in a hooked, parrot-like beak.

Just above the eyes there were two long horns that pointed forward. He looked like a walking army tank with two guns aimed at the enemy. Above the beak and on the nose, a shorter horn stood upright. These three horns gave him the name **Triceratops.** A thick overhang of bone guarded the eyes.

Triceratops was a fierce fighter.

Triceratops

There were other giant ceratopsians in late Cretaceous days. They all belonged to the same family—even though their shields were somewhat different.

Monoclonius (monn-uh-KLONE-e-yuss) had one big horn standing on his nose and a very short, thick horn over each eye. The one large horn gave him his name. In 1876, Professor Cope, whom we spoke about earlier, found an almost complete skeleton of this curious creature in the badlands of Montana.

Chasmosaurus (kaz-muh-SAWR-us) had small horns over the eyes and one on the nose, and a ruffled frill or shield. Openings in the frill gave him his name.

Styracosaurus (sty-RACK-uh-SAWR-us) had a large horn on the nose, and a very short one over each eye. His shield had a frame of spikes which gave him his name.

These strange animals were the last of the dinosaurs. They were a late development and their time on earth was cut short by the great changes that were taking place toward the end of the Mesozoic Era.

Monoclonius

92

Chasmosaurus

Styracosaurus

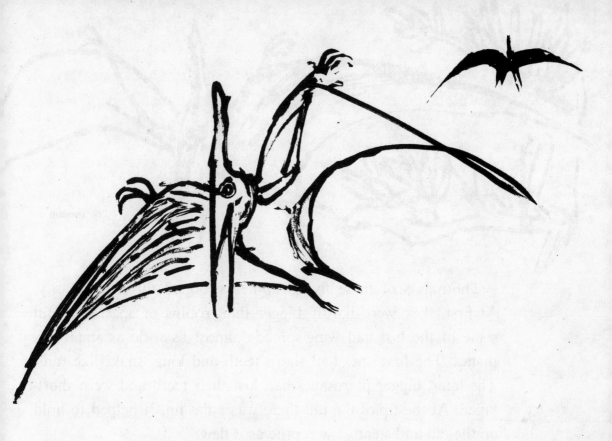

8   *Flying Reptiles*

In Jurassic days, something new happened. Up to that time there were reptiles in the sea and reptiles on the land But now there were also reptiles in the air. These were the pterosaurs (TERR-uh-sawrs), or flying reptiles. Like the dinosaurs, they came from the thecodonts. Pterosaurs lived some 155 to 60 million years ago through the Cretaceous period and then disappeared with their dinosaur cousins.

They are called both pterosaurs ("wing-lizard") and pterodactyls (terr-uh-DACK-tills) ("wing-finger"). Both are good names.

Pteranodon

Thousands of these flying reptiles swooped through the sky. At first, they were hardly bigger than robins or sparrows. But some of the last had wing-spreads almost as wide as small airplanes. The first ones had sharp teeth and long, snake-like tails. The later, bigger pterosaurs had lost their teeth and were short-tailed. At the tip of the tail there was a flat fin. It helped to hold up the tail and steady the reptile as it flew.

The skeleton and body had to change quite a bit for living in the air. The paper-thin bones became hollow, yet very strong.

In all of the pterosaurs, the fingers were small, hook-like claws except the fourth finger which grew very long. They could have used the claws for hanging onto tree branches or rocks. The back legs were not very strong. Pterosaurs probably walked around on the ground very little or not at all.

The wing was a sheet of skin stretched from the long fourth finger to the hind leg. But the flying reptile's wing was not so good as the bat's. A bat has four fingers which help support the wing and make it stronger. The flying reptile had only one finger to support the wing. So if a reptile tore his wing skin, he probably could not fly at all.

94

Scientists believe that reptiles glided or soared through the air rather than flapped their wings. With such wings, the creatures must have found it difficult to lift themselves into the air. It is believed they had to climb up a cliff or tree and take off from there.

Pterosaurs had large brains for reptiles. Just like birds today, their sight was very good. They needed good eyes because their sense of smell was poor. They had to see their prey in order to chase it.

Some scientists believe that flying reptiles might have been partly warm-blooded. Cold-blooded reptiles become tired very easily. Flying reptiles sometimes had to fly for long periods of time with no place to rest and they might have developed a warm-blooded condition like birds and mammals.

8.1 Rhamphorhynchus

Rhamphorhynchus (ram-fuh-RINK-us) was one of the many different kinds of flying reptiles of the Jurassic period. Like most of the first flying reptiles, it had teeth and a long, rudder-like tail.

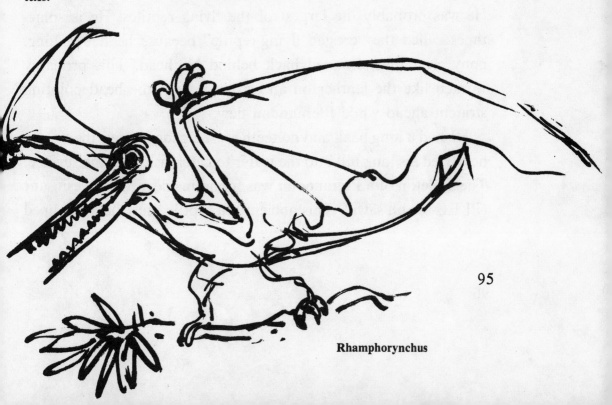

95

Rhamphorynchus

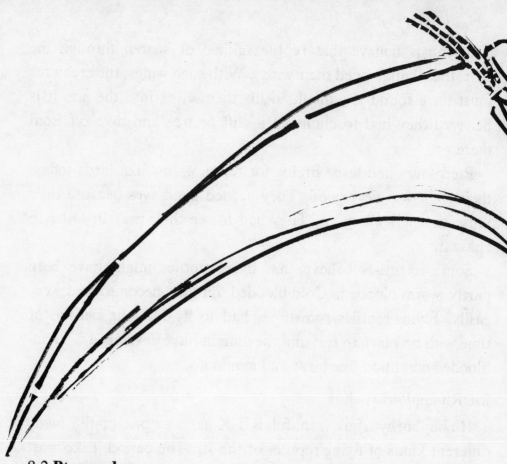

8.2 Pteranodon

Pteranodon (tuh-RAN-uh-donn) lived in the Cretaceous period. He was probably the largest of the flying reptiles. He is sometimes called the "crested flying reptile" because he had a long, bony crest that swooped back behind his head. This probably worked like the feather on an arrow. It kept the head pointing straight ahead while **Pteranodon** flew.

He had a long beak and no teeth. As he glided above the waves, he darted his long bill into the water to catch fish near the surface. The skeleton of a **Pteranodon** was found inside a fossil plesiosaur (PLEE-see-uh-sawr). This ancient sea reptile must have snapped

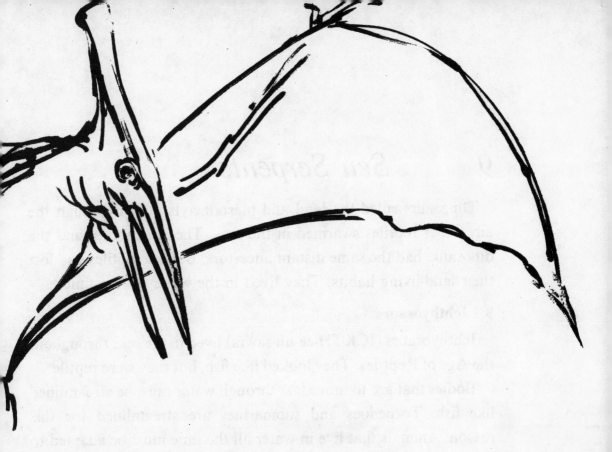

its great jaws over the **Pteranodon** as it glided down to gobble up a small fish.

Pteranodon had a small light body. He probably weighed less than thirty pounds. But his wing spread could reach 27 feet in width. The fossil skeletons of **Pteranodon** found in the chalk beds of Kansas prove that the great wings sometimes carried these animals at least 100 miles over the inland sea that covered Kansas.

Pteranodon did not fly so well as a bat or bird. He could not fold his wings back to dive down and catch some prey.

Some scientists believe that **Pteranodon** used his claws to cling, like a bat, to rocks or trees.

9   Sea Serpents

Dinosaurs ruled the land and pterodactyls glided through the air. Other reptiles swarmed in the seas. The sea reptiles and the dinosaurs had the same distant ancestors. But sea reptiles had lost their land-living habits. They lived in the water all the time.

9.1 Ichthyosaurs

Ichthyosaurs (ICKTH-ee-uh-sawrs) lived in the seas throughout the Age of Reptiles. They looked like fish, but they were reptiles.

Bodies that are to move fast through water must be streamlined like fish. Torpedoes and submarines are streamlined for this reason. Animals that live in water all the time must be adapted to it. Ichthyosaurs spent all their time in water. They looked like the sharks or porpoises of today.

Some ichthyosaurs were quite small, but others were 20 or 30 feet long. They had huge eyes. The long tooth-filled jaws of these reptiles must have been a deadly menace to schools of fish swimming the Jurassic seas. They were sleek, fast swimmers.

The body of an ichthyosaur had a large two-lobed tail which drove the animal through the water. The four legs were fin-shaped and a large back fin, like a shark's, kept the ichthyosaur from rolling over.

98

These water-living reptiles did not lay eggs on land as the dinosaurs did. The eggs stayed in their bodies until the baby ichthyosaurs hatched. Then the young were born alive. They were ovoviviparous (oh-voh-vy-VIPP-uh-russ). Some snakes are ovoviviparous.

We know that ichthyosaurs came from land-living reptiles. For some reason they began to spend more of their time in the water. They lived like fish and their feet were like fins—good for swimming.

A skeleton of an ichthyosaur in the American Museum of Natural History proves this. The skeleton was found near Stuttgart, Germany and is believed to be the most perfect of its kind in the world. It is preserved in a slab of slate. The impression shows several baby animals within the body cavity of the adult ichthyosaur.

Ichthyosaurs are a good example of adaptations of animals. These reptiles developed from animals that lived in the water, but they became adapted to living on land. Then they went back to the sea!

Ichthyosaur

Why the ichthyosaur returned to the water no one knows. It looked like a fish on the outside, but it kept the reptile's brain, bones, heart, and lungs. Whales and porpoises are examples of mammals that returned to the sea. They may look like fish, but they are mammals through and through. The ichthyosaurs were strange in that they looked like fish, and had the body structure of reptiles, yet bore their young alive, like mammals.

9.2 Plesiosaurs

Another kind of reptile that returned to water-living was the plesiosaur (PLEE-see-uh-SAWR). For about 95 million years the Jurassic and Cretaceous seas were full of big and small plesiosaurs.

They probably could have come ashore, like modern seals, to warm themselves in the sun. But they are believed to have been strictly water-living reptiles.

Plesiosaur

The plesiosaurs were not shaped like fish. They had broad, flat turtle-like bodies.

In taking to the water, the leg bones of these reptiles shortened and each set of five toes grew into paddles that were about five-feet long. With these, the plesiosaurs rowed themselves slowly forward or backward.

The Denver Museum of Natural History has a perfect 40 foot skeleton of a plesiosaur. It has a small head, 20 foot neck, and a stubby tail. Indeed, it looks like a long snake strung through the body of a great turtle. The long neck could dart from side to side to capture fish.

Some plesiosaurs had longer heads and shorter necks. But small or large head, the mouth was a fish trap armed with many long, sharp-pointed teeth.

Plesiosaurs flopped up onto the land to lay their eggs. Possibly some of the later dinosaurs and early small mammals found these unprotected eggs to be quite tasty. At any rate, the plesiosaurs disappeared with the dinosaurs at the end of the Cretacous period.

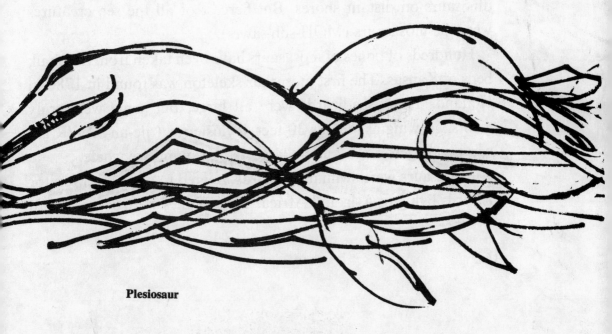

Plesiosaur

9.3 Mosasaurs

During the 60 million years of the Cretaceous period, the warm sea covering Kansas was filled with fierce monsters. Ichthyosaurs darted through the deep waters. Plesiosaurs slowly paddled at the surface snapping at small fish and watching the strange land-living dinosaurs on distant shores. But fiercest of all the sea creatures were the mosasaurs (MOH-suh-sawrs).

Hundreds of bones of mosasaurs have been taken from the chalk beds of Kansas. The first mosasaur skeleton was found in 1780 in Holland. These sea-lizards were all large, but some were truly giants, growing as long as 30 feet. **Tylosaurus** (tile-uh-SAWR-us) was the biggest mosasaur, as large as a medium-size whale.

Mosasaurs were swimming lizards, related to the large Monitor Lizards living in Asia and Africa. Their bodies were covered with

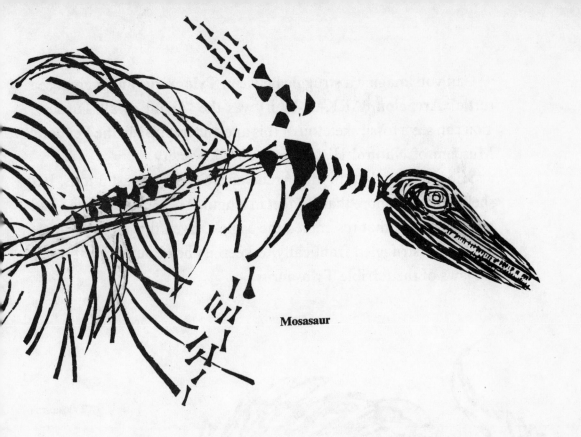

Mosasaur

small overlapping scales. Lizards are a certain kind of reptile that began to appear in late Mesozoic times, some 130 million years ago. The mosasaurs were a family of lizards that left their land-living relatives and returned to the water.

The were adapted to their life in water, but never became quite so fish-like as the ichthyosaurs. The body and tail were long, flexible, and powerful. Balanced by the four paddle-shaped feet, the mosasaur moved swiftly. It was truly a sea serpent.

Vicious teeth lined the pointed jaws. A mosasaur could swallow large fish. This large-mouthed monster must have terrified the smaller animals as it whipped through the Cretaceous seas.

103

Monitor Lizard

Can you imagine a struggle between **Tylosaurus** and a great sea turtle? **Archelon** (ARK-uh-lonn) was the "Giant of all Turtles." You can see a fossil skeleton of this ancient creature in the Peabody Museum of Natural History at Yale University.

Scientists say that, in life, **Archelon** weighed at least 3 tons. His shell measured more than 12 feet in length. The yard-long head had a hooked beak that resembled the eagle's. Even this monster turtle must have struggled frantically to keep its head out of the powerful jaws of the terrible **Tylosaurus.**

Tylosaurus

104

The Yale fossil shows an injured flipper. Do you suppose it was the result of a battle between the giant **Archelon** and the terrible **Tylosaurus?**

Mosasaurs lived about 75 million years ago. We sometimes hear stories of sea serpents today. Scientists usually find that people have really seen sharks, whales, sea lions or other animals. Mosasaurs were certainly like the great monsters of the deep told in stories. But the mosasaurs all disappeared millions of years ago with the dinosaurs, ichthyosaurs, and plesiosaurs.

Slowly, the land beneath the seas they swam lifted up. The seas became lakes, then disappeared. The mosasaurs lived for only a short time on earth compared with the other giant reptiles, but the story of their life, too, can be read from the fossils left in rocks.

Archelon

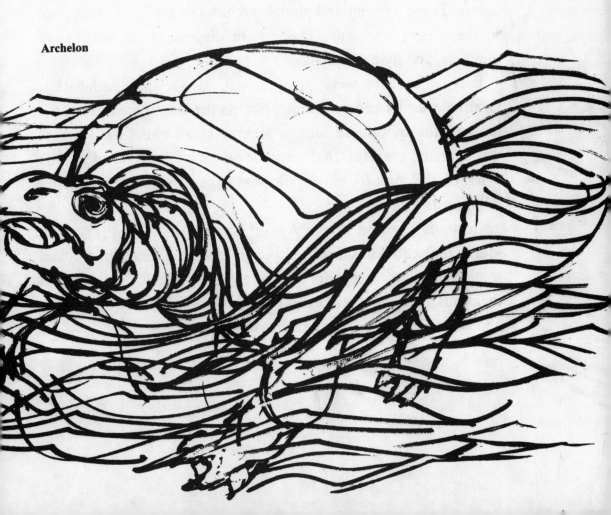

10   *Adaptations of Dinosaurs*

In the days of dinosaurs, as now, there was a "balance of nature." There were many kinds of plants and animals and each had its place and purpose in nature's plan.

There were big and little plant-eaters that fed on the green plants. There were big and little flesh-eaters that fed on the plant-eaters. There were upland plants and animals and those that lived in the watery lowlands. There were diggers in the earth, tree climbers, and flying animals.

Early dinosaurs were small, swift, two-legged flesh-eaters. **Ornitholestes** looked very much like its thecodont ancestors as it scurried through dense jungles seeking small game for food. It was light and graceful. In the middle period of dinosaurs days, the place of this fleet-footed reptile was taken by the much larger **Allosaurus.**

In the last period of the Age of Reptiles the giant **Tyrannosaurus** replaced **Allosaurus.** Although these two dinosaurs looked somewhat alike, except for size, there were many differences in their muscles and bones. **Tyrannosaurus'** back legs became bigger and stronger and the feet became broader.

Dinosaurs lived in all kinds of surroundings. The upland forms developed bodies that were good for moving about on hard ground. The two-legged flesh-eaters and also many of the four-legged horned and armored dinosaurs lived on the dry land.

Many dinosaurs spent most of their time in the swamps and marshes of the lowlands. Their bodies adapted in many different ways to this kind of water life. Giant sauropods, like **Bronto-saurus,** developed strong, yet light bones to support their huge bodies.

Others had nostrils on the tops of their heads. This change allowed the animal to breathe while floating in the water with only part of the head above the surface.

In Cretaceous days, the duck-billed dinosaurs were even better equipped for living in the water. Their feet were webbed and their narrow tails helped them swim.

Some duck-bills developed air storage crests on their heads.

Some dinosaurs may have even climbed trees. **Hypsilophodon** (hips-ih-LOFF-uh-dunn) was a small Jurassic dinosaur. It had grasping feet that seem to be adapted for holding onto branches.

All dinosaurs developed teeth to fit their eating habits. **Allosaurus** and **Tyrannosaurus** had wide, gaping mouths filled with sharp dagger-like teeth that were used for tearing the flesh of their prey.

Giant plant-eaters, like **Brontosaurus,** had only a few peg-like teeth in the front parts of their jaws. The teeth of many duck-bills could grind food into an oatmeal-like mash. Then there was **Struthiomimus** with no teeth at all.

Even the jaws of the dinosaurs were adapted to certain eating habits. In the lizard-like hipped dinosaurs, the jaws worked like scissors. The upper and lower teeth slid past each other as they bit. With this type of jaw the flesh-eaters were able to tear and cut their victims into chunks that could be swallowed.

It is interesting to know that even though the toothless, fruit-eating **Struthiomimus** no longer ate meat, it still kept the jaw it inherited from its thecodont ancestors. The giant sauropods, like **Brontosaurus,** also kept the same scissor-like jaw. They did little, if any, chewing of food and didn't need another kind of jaw.

The bird-like hipped dinosaurs had jaws that worked like nut-crackers. The teeth clamped together all at once. These dinosaurs could cut and chop and sometimes even grind their food before swallowing it.

Dinosaurs kept up a never-ending battle between the hunters and the hunted. Some dinosaurs developed weapons for defense. Spikes, club-like tails, horns, and thick plates helped protect

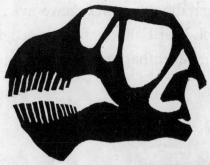

Flesh-eater's Teeth   **Plant-eater's Teeth**

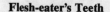

many plant-eaters. Some dinosaurs developed thick, solid skulls that possibly protected their tiny brains.

The warm climate of Mesozoic days helped some dinosaurs to grow into giants. Plants grew thickly everywhere. The dinosaurs thrived and grew and grew. But living comfortably in the warm days and eating all they could stuff into themselves was not enough to make these reptiles as big as railroad cars.

All living things have limits to their size. In backboned animals a little gland at the base of the brain holds a certain chemical that makes animals grow. It is called the pituitary (pih-TU-ih-terry) gland. If a human being or other animal grows much larger than the average height for his race, his pituitary gland is probably overactive. An underactive pituitary gland makes a dwarf. A large pituitary gland also may be the cause of "giantism." Scientists have discovered that the giant dinosaur had an unusually large pituitary gland compared with the size of the rest of the brain.

No one knows whether or not dinosaurs made any sound. We know that other reptiles of today make sounds. Snakes hiss and alligators can growl fiercely. Whether or not dinosaurs hissed, growled or bellowed when frightened or angry, no one knows.

Also, we do not know about the color of dinosaurs' skins. But we do know that most animals today have a skin or fur that blends with the kind of area they live in. Tree snakes in tropical jungles are patterned in such a way that, unless they move, you can hardly see them against the leaves. Alligators blend in so well with

Bony Plates   **Spikes**   109

the floor of a tropical jungle that you could easily tread on one if you did not watch you step.

Dinosaurs may have had a protective skin coloring, too. This could have helped the harmless **Camptosaurus** survive in a land of flesh-eaters. Something favored **Camptosaurus.** He lasted into the Cretaceous period. That is more than can be said for some other well-known Jurassic dinosaurs.

In Cretaceous days, North America had changed. It was only semi-tropical. Palms and ferns grew along the shores of rivers, lakes, and inland seas. But the uplands were slowly pushing up, higher and higher.

It was the last period of the Age of Reptiles when the dinosaurs changed into many strange forms to fit the changing world.

Struthiomimus, the "ostrich dinosaur," played about the same part in Cretaceous days as **Camptosaurus** did in Jurassic days. **Struthiomimus** lived on tiny animals and plants, too.

In the beginning of the Cretaceous period, **Gorgosaurus** was the new tyrant flesh-eater. He was bigger and faster than **Allosaurus.** But in the last part of the period, **Tyrannosaurus rex** was the King of Tyrants, the biggest and fiercest of all.

As in Jurassic days, there were the hunters and the hunted, flesh-eaters and plant-eaters, big and little animals, dry land and water forms. They all managed to live together. This is called the "balance of nature."

There must be many kinds of animals to keep the balance of nature. When you think of how each kind of dinosaur filled a certain role when it lived, it is easier to understand why there were so many strange forms of life on earth.

11   The Dinosaur Mystery

No one really knows why all the dinosaurs disappeared. But scientists have found some very interesting clues to the mystery. They know that many things happened to make life difficult for these strange creatures.

The Age of Reptiles was finished at the end of the Cretaceous period, 60 million years ago. It did not happen overnight. We know that the dinosaurs roamed over the earth for some 140 million years. Like many other forms of fossil animals, dinosaurs began as rather small creatures. As the years passed, they grew larger and developed into many strange forms.

Some of the armored dinosaurs turned into fantastic shapes with spikes, bumps and warts all over their bodies.

One of the reasons for their disappearance may have had something to do with the inner make-up of the dinosaurs' bodies. Many dinosaurs had very large pituitary glands and very large bodies. The great monsters ate tons of food each day. The pituitary gland may have done more to the dinosaurs' bodies than make them gigantic. It may have harmfully affected them in other ways. Not all dinosaurs were giants, so this reason could have affected only some kinds.

Perhaps dinosaurs were too stupid to survive. Their brains were very small and not much good for thinking. If food became scarce, their tiny brains could not help them find new ways of getting it.

Scientists have compared the weights of several animals' bodies with the weights of their brains. A man's body is about 50 times the weight of his brain. A dog weighs 110 times more than its brain, and an elephant, 1000 times. A large dinosaur probably would have weighed from 25,000 to 50,000 times the weight of its brain. Dinosaurs were certainly more stupid than any mammal we know today.

Near the end of the Age of Reptiles new enemies arrived. They were the little furry mammals. No bigger than rats, the little fellows had two things in their favor. They had large brains and were smarter than the great reptiles. The mammals were warm-blooded and lived easily and comfortably on land. The cold-blooded dinosaurs had to move more slowly. They tired faster in moving about on land. The mammals were quick and clever compared with the sluggish dinosaurs.

Many mammals are active night hunters. It is possible that quick, brainy little animals learned to feed on unprotected dinosaur eggs. As more mammals began to scurry around and eat

more and more of the dinosaur eggs, fewer and fewer of the great reptiles were born. This loss of young might have helped in the final disappearance of all dinosaurs.

Now we come to, perhaps, the most important reason for the death of the dinosaurs.

The dinosaurs lived at a time when the earth was low and flat. Great seas and swamps covered the earth. The air was hot and humid. The dinosaurs were at home in this world. There was plenty of food to fill the great stomach cavities of the plant-eaters. And there were plenty of big plant-eaters to satisfy the hunger of the meat-eaters.

But then something happened. The earth began pushing upward in spots. It was the birth of the great mountain systems, like our Rockies. The lowlands slowly gave way to rolling uplands. Hardwood forests began to grow where ferns and palms grew before. Temperate and cold areas gradually replaced the world-wide tropical climate of earlier Mesozoic days.

Such great changes did not take place overnight. No dinosaur stood at the edge of his swamp and watched the mountains push up. It took thousands of years.

Mammals

But slowly and steadily the earth was changing. After a long time, it began to affect the dinosaurs. Swamps, lakes and rivers where the plant-eaters lived grew smaller. The tremendous amounts of food they needed began to disappear. They could not think or move far enough to find new feeding grounds.

Although these changes took place slowly, they happened too fast for the dinosaurs. The plant-eaters could not find a diet that would have allowed them to live in the new world.

As the plant-eaters died, the flesh-eaters lost their great food supply. Giants, like **Tyrannosaurus rex,** needed tons of meat to keep alive. Mammals were too tiny and too active for the slower reptiles to feed on.

All of these things made it harder and harder for dinosaurs to survive. It seems strange that a few of the smaller kinds did not live on. But, it seems, none were able to adapt themselves to the new world.

Other reptiles, too, failed to survive the changes taking place on earth during Cretaceous days. The flying reptiles disappeared. So did the water-dwelling plesiosaurs, ichthyosaurs and mosasaurs. No one knows why sea reptiles did not continue to live in the seas that did not dry up.

114

A few kinds of reptiles did survive—our snakes, turtles and crocodiles of today. But the day of the giant reptiles was over. They lived for a long time. And they lived well. But all that remains to tell us of their wonderful story are the fossils we chip from the rock that has enclosed them for millions of years.

List of North American Museums

1 Academy of Natural Sciences, Philadelphia, Pennsylvania.

First *Hadrosaurus* skeleton found in North America. Many fine sea reptiles collected in England about 100 years ago.

2 American Museum of Natural History, New York City, New York.

Greatest display of fossil reptiles in the world. Has many dinosaur skeletons and skulls. Also many early reptiles, mammal-like reptiles, thecodonts, turtles, crocodilians, ichthyosaurs, plesiosaurs and pterosaurs.

3 Amherst College Museum, Amherst, Massachusetts.

Duck-billed dinosaur skeleton, *Trachodon*.

4 California Institute of Technology, Pasadena, California.

Fossil reptiles from Pacific coast area.

5 Carnegie Museum, Pittsburgh, Pennsylvania.

Jurassic dinosaurs from Morrison formation of Utah.

6 Chicago Natural History Museum, Chicago, Illinois.

Many dinosaurs.

7 Colorado Museum of Natural History, Denver, Colorado.

Diplodocus, Trachodon, Stegosaurus, Mosasaurus skeletons. Skulls of *Troödon* and flesh-eater.

8 Dyche Museum of the University of Kansas, Lawrence, Kansas.

Cretaceous mosasaurs collected in Kansas.

9 Museum of Comparative Zoology of Harvard University, Cambridge, Mass.

Many Permian fossils, and sea reptiles.

10 Museum of Paleontology of the University of California, Berkeley, Calif.

Fossil reptiles from Pacific coast area and southern United States. Triassic reptiles from Arizona, and Cretaceous forms from California.

11 Museum of Paleontology of the University of Michigan, Ann Arbor, Mich.

Permian and Triassic amphibians and reptiles found in Texas.

12 National Museum of Canada, Ottawa, Canada.

Many Cretaceous dinosaurs found in western Canada.

13 Peabody Museum of Yale University, New Haven, Connecticut.

Many fine dinosaur skeletons.

14 Royal Ontario Museum, Toronto, Canada.

Many late Cretaceous dinosaurs found in Alberta, Canada.

15 United States National Museum, Washington, D. C.

Many dinosaurs, some of which were collected by Professor Marsh. Also early reptiles, turtles, and fossil lizards.

16 Utah Field House of Natural History, Vernal, Utah.

Dinosaur remains from Vernal area. Many fine displays.

17 Walker Museum of the University of Chicago, Chicago, Illinois.

Many dinosaurs.

Appendix B.

Selected References

Andrews, Roy Chapman. *All About Dinosaurs*. New York: Random House, 1953.

Andrews, Roy Chapman. "Explorations in the Gobi Desert." *National Geographic Magazine*. June, 1933.

Bird, Roland T. "We Captured a Live Brontosaurus." *National Geographic Magazine*. May, 1954.

Colbert, Edwin H. *The Dinosaur Book*. New York: McGraw-Hill for the American Museum of Natural History. 1951.

Hegner, Robert. *Parade of the Animal Kingdom*. New York: Macmillan, 1944.

Hughes Tool Research Division Collection on Ancient Fauna and Flora painted by John Pemberton Cowan. Hughes Tool Company, P. O. Box 2539, Houston 1, Texas.

Knight, Charles R. *Before the Dawn of History*. New York: McGraw-Hill Book Company. 1935.

Knight, Charles R. "Parade of Life Through the Ages." *National Geographic Magazine*. February, 1942.

Look, Al. *1,000 Million Years on the Colorado Plateau*. Denver: Bell Publishings, Denver, Colorado. 1955.

Lull, Richard S. *The Sauropod Dinosaur Borosaurus Marsh*. New Haven, Conn.: Yale University Press. 1919.

Parker, Bertha Morris. Basic Science Series. Evanston, Ill.: Row, Peterson Company.
Animals of Yesterday. 1950.
Frogs and Toads. 1945.
Life Through the Ages. 1950.
Reptiles. 1950.
Stories Read from Rocks. 1950.

Parker, Bertha Morris. *The Golden Book of Science*. New York: Simon & Schuster. 1956.

Romer, Alfred S. *Vertebrate Paleontology*. Chicago: University of Chicago Press. 1945.

Schuchert, Charles and Carl O. Dunbar. *A Textbook of Geology —Part II—Historical Geology*. New York: John Wiley & Sons Inc. 1941.

Simpson, George Gaylord. *Life of the Past*. Connecticut: Yale University Press, 1953.

Wyler, Rose and G. Ames. *Animals of the Past—Stamps. A Golden Play Book*. New York: Simon & Schuster. 1954.

Zim, Herbert S. *Dinosaurs*. New York: Wm. Morrow & Company. 1954.

Pronouncing Dictionary and Index

Lived in late Jurassic and early Cretaceous periods; Ornithischian, small plant-eating dinosaur with rounded bird-like beak, 71-72, 73, 78, 110.

Canada, 32, 82, 87.

National Museum of, 116.

Carnegie Museum, Pittsburgh, Pennsylvania, 32, 116.

Carnivores (CAR-nih-vors) flesh eaters, 5.

Ceratopsians (serr-uh-TOPS-e-yunns. From Greek, *keras, keratos* — "horn" + *ops* — "face". The horned dinosaurs.) 8, 48, 71, 87-88, 92.

Chasmosaurus (kaz-muh-SAWR-us. From Greek, *chasma* — "opening" + *sauros* — "lizard", named because of openings in the frill of this horned dinosaur.) Lived in late Cretaceous period; Ornithischian, giant plant-eating, armored dinosaur, with small horns over eyes and nose, ruffled frill over neck, 92.

Chicago, Natural History Museum, 116.

Civil War, 31.

Climate, 13, 15, 61, 110.

Coelacanth (SEE-luh-kanth). Both an ancient and a recent lobe-finned fish; a fossil of Devonian to Cretaceous periods, and recent ones found living in seas near Africa; belonged to crossopterygian family, related to lung-fish and an ancestor of amphibians, 35.

Colorado Museum of Natural History, Denver, 116.

Connecticut, 20, 29.

Connecticut, Peabody Museum of Yale University, 116.

Cope, Edward D., 31.

Corythosaurus (KOR-ith-uh-SAWR-us. From Greek, *korythos* — "helmet" + *sauros* — "lizard", named because of helmet-like crest on head.) Lived in late Cretaceous period; Ornithischian, large plant-eater, duck-billed dinosaur with crested head, 75, 83.

Cotylosaurs (KOTT-ih-luh-SAWRS. From Greek, *kotyles* — "cup" + *sauros* — "lizard", named because back bones were each shaped like cups.)

Lived in Permian and Triassic periods; among first reptiles; early ones were flesh-eaters, later ones were plant-eaters, with a "third eye" like the Tuatara lizard today, 41-42.

Crests in trachodont dinosaurs, 81-84.

Cretaceous (kree-TAY-shuss) period, the third and latest of the periods included in the Mesozoic era, began about 120 million and ended 60 million years ago, lasted about 60 million years, 48.

Cretaceous dinosaurs, kinds and activities of, 110.

Crossopterygian fishes (cross-opp-tuh-RIDJ-e-yunn. From Greek, *krossoi* — "tassels or fringe" + pteryz — "wing or fin".) Devonian period; medium size, lobe-finned fishes in which bones in their fins were arranged like bones in the limbs of their descendants that were the first land-living vertebrates, 35.

Cuvier, Baron Georges, 28.

Cynognathus (sih-NOGG-nuh-thuss. From Greek, *kyon, kynos* — "dog" + *gnathus* — "jaws", named because of dog-like shape of jaws.) Lived in Triassic period; small or medium-size flesh-eater, part reptile, part mammal; link between cold-blooded reptiles and warm-blooded mammals, 42.

Defense weapons of dinosaurs, 108, 109.

Denver, Colorado Museum of Natural History, 101, 116.

Deserts, 22, 40, 41.

Devonian (deh-VOH-nih-yunn) period, the fourth in order of age of the periods of Paleozoic era, between Silurian and Mississippian periods; also called Age of Fishes; began about 300 million and ended 235 million years ago, lasted 65 million years, 11, 12.

Diet of Dinosaurs, 51, 52, 70, 78, 79.

Dinosaur National Monument, Vernal, Utah, 32, 64.

Dinosaurs (DY-nuh-sawrs. From Greek, *dienos* — "terrible" + *sauros* — "lizard".) Lived in Mesozoic era, 200 million to 60 million years ago; common name for two great orders of extinct cold-blooded reptiles, Saurischians and Ornithischians.

Diplocaulus (dip-luh-KAWL-us. From Greek, *diploos* — "double" + *kaulos* — "shaft or stalk".) Lived in Permian period; water-living amphibian with head shaped like tremendously broad arrowhead, 37.

Diplodocus (dih-PLODD-uh-kuss. From Greek, *diploos* — "double" + *dokos* — "beam", named for double spines on backbones.) Lived in Jurassic period; Saurischian, giant plant-eating dinosaur, with nostrils on top of head, 47, 66, 67.

Duck-billed dinosaurs, see **Trachodon**.

Dyche Museum of the University of Kansas, Lawrence, 116.

Era (EAR-uh). Large division of geologic time, having one or more periods; includes Archeozoic, Proterozoic, Paleozoic, Mesozoic, and Cenozoic eras, 11-12.

Eryops (ERR-ee-ops. From Greek *eryein* — "to draw out" + *ops* — "face", named because most of skull is in front of the eyes.) Lived in Permian period; large land-living amphibian with four strong legs, 37.

Fossils (FOSS-ills). The remains or traces of animals or plants preserved by natural causes in rocks.

Gastroliths (GAS-truh-liths). Stones swallowed by dinosaurs to help them digest food; well rounded, highly polished by their stomach juices, 64-65.

Gizzard stones. See Gastroliths.

Gobi Desert, 32, 40-41, 87-89.

Gorgosaurus (gor-guh-SAWR-us. From Greek, *gorgos* — "terrible" + *sauros* — "lizard".) Lived in Cretaceous period; Saurischian, medium-size flesh-eating land-living dinosaur, 56.

Growth of dinosaurs, 54, 61, 109.

Mammal-like reptiles, 42.

Mantell, Gideon, 28, 73.

Marine reptiles, see Sea Serpents.

Marsh, Othniel Charles, 31.

Megalosaurus (MEGG-uh-luh-SAWR-us). Lived in early Jurassic period; Saurischian, flesh-eater, ancestor of **Allosaurus**, 52.

Mesozoic (mess-uh-ZO-ick) era. One of the grand divisions or eras of geologic time; between Paleozoic and Cenozoic eras; contains Triassic, Jurassic, and Cretaceous periods; known as Age of Dinosaurs; began 200 million and ended 60 million years ago, lasted 140 million years, 12, 21, 48.

Michigan, Museum of the University, 116.

Mineralization, 19.

Mississippian (mis-sis-SIP-ih-yunn) period. Fifth of seven periods of Paleozoic era; between Devonian and Pennsylvanian periods; Age of Amphibians; began about 290 million and ended 260 million years ago, lasted about 30 million years, 12.

Monitor (MONN-ih-terr) lizards, large lizards now living in Asia and Africa, 102, 103.

Monoclonius (monn-uh-KLONE-e-yuss. From Greek, *monoklonos* — "with a single stem", named because of one large horn on head.) Lived in Cretaceous period; Ornithischian, giant plant-eating, armored dinosaur with short horns over eyes and one large horn on nose, 92.

Montana, 14, 20, 32.

Moody, Pliny, 30.

Mosasaurs (MOH-suh-sawrs. From Latin and Greek, *mosa* — the Meuse River in Belgium where first specimen was found + *sauros* — "lizard".) Lived in Cretaceous period; giant sea lizards; long bodies and tails, pointed jaws were filled with sharp teeth, 102-105.

Museums, fossils in, 24-25.

  list of, 116-117.

Museum of Comparative Zoology of Harvard University, 116.

Museum of Paleontology of University of California, 116.

Museum of Paleontology of University of Michigan, 116.

New York, American Museum of Natural History, 32, 40, 89, 99.

Nodosaurus (no-duh-SAWR-us. From Greek, *nodos* — "toothless" + *sauros* — "lizard".) Lived in Cretaceous period; Ornithischian, medium-size plant-eating, armored dinosaur, 86.

Opal, 21.

Ordovician (or-doe-VISH-yunn) period. Second period of Paleozoic era; between Cambrian and Silurian periods; began about 250 million and ended 175 million years ago, lasted 75 million years, 12.

Ornithischian (or-nih-THISK-e-yunn. From Greek, *ornis, ornithos* — "bird" + *ischion* — "hip", named because hip bones are like a bird's. Lived in Jurassic and Cretaceous periods; one of the two great orders of dinosaurs, plant-eating; includes duck-billed, armored, and horned dinosaurs, 46, 48, 68-92.

Ornitholestes (OR-nith-uh-LESS-teez. From Greek, *ornis, ornithos* — "bird" + *lestes* — "robber", named because some scientists imagined it as catching early birds.) Lived in Jurassic period; Saurischian, small flesh-eating dinosaur, 52-53, 60, 106.

Ornithopods (OR-nith-uh-PODDS.) Lived in Cretaceous period; Ornithischian, plant-eating, duck-billed dinosaurs, walked on two or four feet, 48, 71.

Ostrich dinosaur, see **Struthiomimus.**

Oviraptor (oh-vih-RAPP-terr. Greek, *ovo* — "egg" + *raptor* — "snatches", named because it is believed to have lived by sucking eggs of other dinosaurs.) Lived in Cretaceous period; small dinosaur, 40.

Ovoviviparous (oh-voh-vy-VIPP-uh-russ) dinosaurs, water-living reptiles that kept eggs inside their bodies, young were born alive in water, 99.

Owen, Sir Richard, 28.

Pachycephalosaurus (pack-uh-SEFF-uh-luh-SAWR-us. From Greek, *packys* — "thickness" + *kephalon* — "head" + *sauros* — "lizard", named because of thick skull.) Lived in late Cretaceous period; Ornithischian, small plant-eating duck-billed dinosaur, bone at top of head was 10 inches thick, 84.

Paleontology (PAY-lee-yon-TAHL-uh-jee. From Greek, *palaios* — "ancient" + *on, onta* — "beings" + *logia* — "to speak".) Science of ancient animal and plant life, 27, 31.

Paleoscincus (PAY-lee-uh-SKINK-us. From Greek, *palaios* — "ancient" + *skinkos* — "lizard", named because teeth look like those of today's skink.) Lived in Cretaceous period; Ornithischian, medium-size, plant-eating dinosaur, armored from head to tail with sharp spikes, 70, 86.

Paleozoic (PAY-lee-uh-ZO-ick). One of the grand eras of geologic time; between Proterozic and Mesozoic; contains Cambrian, Ordovician, Silurian, Devonian, Mississippian, Pennsylvanian, and Permian periods; land plants, amphibians, and reptiles first appeared in later periods; began about 550 million and ended 200 million years ago, lasted 350 million years, 12, 34.

Parasaurolophus (PAR-uh-sawr-AH-luh-fuss. From Greek, *para* — "besides" + *sauros* — "lizard" + *lophos* — "crest".) Lived in Cretaceous period. Ornithischian, medium-size, plant-eating, water-loving, duck-billed dinosaur; had a long air storage chamber on top of head, 75, 83.

Pasadena, California Institute of Technology, 116.

Peabody Museum of Yale University, 104, 116.

Pennsylvanian period, the sixth in order of age of periods of Paleozoic era; between Mississippian and Permian periods; Age of Amphibians; began about 325 million and ended 305 million years ago, lasted 20 million years, 12.

Permian (PURR-mih-yunn) period. Last period of Paleozoic era; beginning of Age of Reptiles; began about 225 million and ended 200 million years ago, lasted 25 million years, 12.

Petrified forests, 18, 19.

Philadelphia, Academy of Natural Sciences, 31, 116.

Pittsburgh, Carnegie Museum, 32, 116.

Pituitary (pih-TU-ih-terry) gland of dinosaurs. A small gland at the base of the brain containing a chemical that makes animals grow, 109, 111.

Plants, 13, 21, 61, 76.

Plant-eating dinosaurs, 6, 51, 61-67, 68-92.

Plant fossils, 18, 19.

Plateosaurus (PLATT-ee-uh-SAWR-us. From Greek, *plata* — "flat" + *sauros* —"lizard".) Lived in Triassic period; Saurischian, medium-size plant-eating dinosaur; walked on two feet, came down on four feet to feed, a link between flesh eaters and giant plant eaters, 61-62.

Plesiosaurs (PLEE-see-uh-SAWRS. From Greek, *plesios* — "near" + *sauros* — "lizard", named because it was thought to be closely related to lizards.) Appeared in late Triassic period and lived through Jurassic and Cretaceous periods; water-living reptiles, fish-eating, looked like snakes strung through turtle bodies, 29, 96, 100-101.

Porpoise (PORE-puss). Water-living mammal, fish-like hairless body, 98.

Preparation of fossils, 23-25.

Protection, means of, 70, 81, 84-87, 91.

Proterozoic (PROTT-urr-uh-ZO-ick) era between Archeozoic and Paleozoic eras; fossils show algae and worms appearing in this era, 12.

Protoceratops (pro-toh-SERR-uh-tops. From Greek, *protos* — "first" + *keratos* — "horn" + *ops* — "face", the first of horned dinosaurs.) Lived in

Cretaceous period; Ornithischian, small plant-eating, had a parrot-like beak and large bony shield over neck, 88.

Psittacosaurus (SIT - uh - kuh - SAWR - us. From Greek, *psittakos* — "parrot" + *sauros* — "lizard", named because of head shape.) Lived in early Cretaceous period; Ornithischian, small plant-eating, horned dinosaur, parrot-shaped head, 88.

Pteranodon (tuh - RAN - uh - donn. From Greek, *pteron* — "wing" + *anodous, anodontos* — "without teeth".) Lived in Cretaceous period; toothless flying reptile, 96-97.

Pterodactyls (terr-uh-DACK-tills. From Greek, *pteron* — "wing" + *dactylos* — "finger", named because wing was supported by fourth finger.) Lived in Jurassic and Cretaceous periods; small short-tailed flying reptiles, 93.

Pterosaurs (TERR-uh-sawrs) Lived in Jurassic and Cretaceous periods; flying reptiles, 29, 48, 93, 94, 95.

Red Deer River, Canada, 82.
Reptiles, Age of, 5, 11-13.
    cold-blooded, 13, 38.
    family tree, of (illustration), 49.
    first, 12, 38-42.
    kinds of, 38-39.
    flying, 93-97.
    mammal-like, 42.
    sea, 48, 98-105.

Rhamphorynchus (ram - fuh - RINK - us. From Greek, *ramphos* — "prow" + *rynchos* — "beak".) Lived in Jurassic period; long-tailed flying reptile, 95.

Rocks, 16-25.
Rocky Mountains, 14, 18, 31, 87, 113.
Royal Ontario Museum, Toronto, Canada, 116.

Sand, 20, 21.
Sandstone, 21.
Sandstorms, 40, 41.

Saurischians (sawr-ISS-kee-yunns. From Greek, *sauros* — "lizard" + *ischion* — "hip", named because hip bones were like a reptile's.) Lived in Triassic through Cretaceous periods; one of two great orders of dinosaurs; includes flesh-eaters and giant plant-eaters, 46, 47, 50-67.

Saurolophus (sawr - AH - luh - fuss. From Greek, *sauros* — "lizard" + *lophos* — "crest".) Lived in Cretaceous period, Ornithischian, large plant-eating, duck-billed dinosaur, bony crest on head, 75, 82.

Sauropods (SAWR-uh-podds). Lived in Jurassic and Cretaceous periods; Saurischian, many were largest plant-eaters, 47, 51, 61-67.

Scientific names, 46, 48.
Sea lizards, mosasaurs, 9, 102.
Sea Serpents, 48, 98-105, 114.
Shale, 19.
Shellac, 23.
Silurian (sih-LURE-ih-yunn) period. Third period of Paleozoic era; between Ordovician and Devonian periods; began about 375 million and ended 345 million years ago, lasted 35 million years, fossils show much coral-reef building, 12.

Size of dinosaurs, 52, 61, 109.
Skin, fossilized, 20, 79, 80, 82, 83.
Slate, 19.
Soft parts, fossilized, 20.
South Africa, 32.
South American, see Galapagos Islands.
Stegosaurs (STEGG-uh-sawrs). Lived in Jurassic; Ornithiscian, large plant-eating armored dinosaurs, 48, 71, 84.

Stegosaurus (STEGG-uh-sawr-us. From Greek, *stegein* — "cover" + *sauros* — "lizard", named because of armor on back.) Lived in Jurassic period; Ornithiscian, large, plant-eating dinosaur with alternate rows of triangular plates down middle of back, four spikes at end of tail, 7, 84-85.

Sternberg, Charles H., 79.

Struthiomimus (STROOTH-ee-uh-MIME-us. From Greek, *strouthion* — "ostrich" + *mimos* — "an imitator", named because it looked like an ostrich.) Lived in late Cretaceous period; Saurischian, medium-size, flesh-eating dinosaur with flat horny beak; probably also ate some plants, 60, 108, 110.

Styracosaurus (sty-RACK-uh-SAWR-us. From Greek, *styrax* — "spike" + *sauros* — "lizard", named from spikes around neck frill.) Lived in Cretaceous period; Ornithischian, giant horned dinosaur, plant-eating, 92.

Sub-fossils, 19.

Sussex, England, 28.

Tail of ichthyosaur (illustrated).

Teeth and jaws of dinosaurs, 108.

Territorial surveys of United States, 31.

Texas, 20, 32.

Thecodonts (THEEK-uh-donnts). Lived in Triassic period; small, ancestors of dinosaurs, 43, 46, 47, 93.

Theropods (THEER-uh-podds). Lived in Triassic through Cretaceous periods; Saurischian, flesh-eating dinosaurs, 47, 51-60.

Thunder Lizard, see **Brontosaurus.**

Toads and frogs, 36.

Toronto, Canada, Royal Ontario Museum, 116.

Trachodon (TRACK - uh - donn. From Greek, *trachys* — "rough" + *odon* — "tooth".) Lived in late Cretaceous period; Ornithischian, large, plant-eating, water-loving, duck-billed dinosaur, 6, 72, 75-81.

Tree-climbing dinosaurs, see **Hypsilophodon.**

Triassic (try - ASS - ick) period. First period of Mesozoic era; early dinosaur forms appeared; began 200 million and ended 155 million years ago, lasted 45 million years, 46, 48, 51.

Triceratops (try-SERR-uh-tops. From Greek, *treis* — "three" + *keras* — "horn" + *ops* — "face".) Lived in Cretaceous period; Ornithiscian, giant, plant-eating, last of horned dinosaurs, three horns on face, 70, 90-91.

Troödon (TRO-uh-donn. From Greek, *troo* — "to wound" + *odon* — "tooth", named because of sharp teeth.) Lived in Cretaceous period; Ornithischian, small or medium-size, plant-eating, duck-billed dinosaurs, with very thick skull bone and spikes and points back of the head, 72, 83-84.

Turtles, see **Archelon.**

Tylosaurus (tile - uh - SAWR - us. From Greek, *tylos* — "a knot" + *sauros* — "lizard".) Lived in Cretaceous period; giant sea lizard, 102-105.

Tyrannosaurus rex (tih-RAN-uh-SAWR-us rex. From Greek, *tyrannos* — "tyrant" + *sauros* — "lizard" + Latin *rex* — "king".) Lived in Cretaceous period; Saurischian, giant, fiercest of flesh-eaters, huge head and jaws, 6, 47, 52, 56-59, 86-87, 106, 108, 110, 114.

United States National Museum, Washington, D.C., 116.

Upland dinosaurs, 107.

Utah, 32.

Utah Field House of Natural History, Vernal, 117.

Vernal, Utah, 32.

Vertebrates (VERR-tuh-brates). Animals with backbones, 34, 35.

Volcanic rocks, 21.

Walker Museum of the University of Chicago, 117.

Washington, D.C. United States National Museum, 117.

Where dinosaurs are found, (illustration).

Wings, (illustration).

Wyoming, 14, 32.

Yale University Museum, 104, 116.

2989